Cindy Sherman
Centerfold
(Untitled #96)

GWEN ALLEN

THE MUSEUM OF MODERN ART, NEW YORK

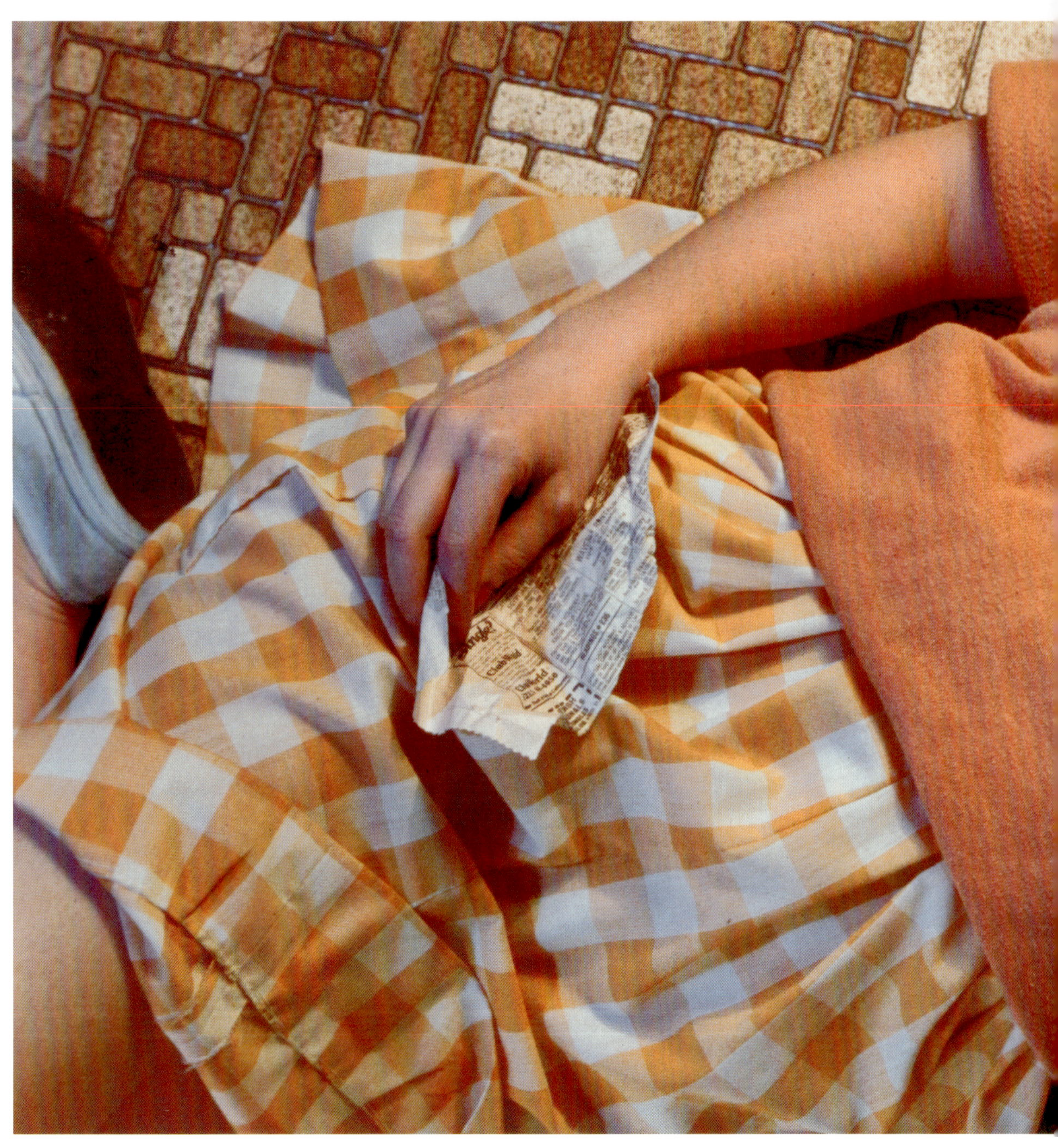

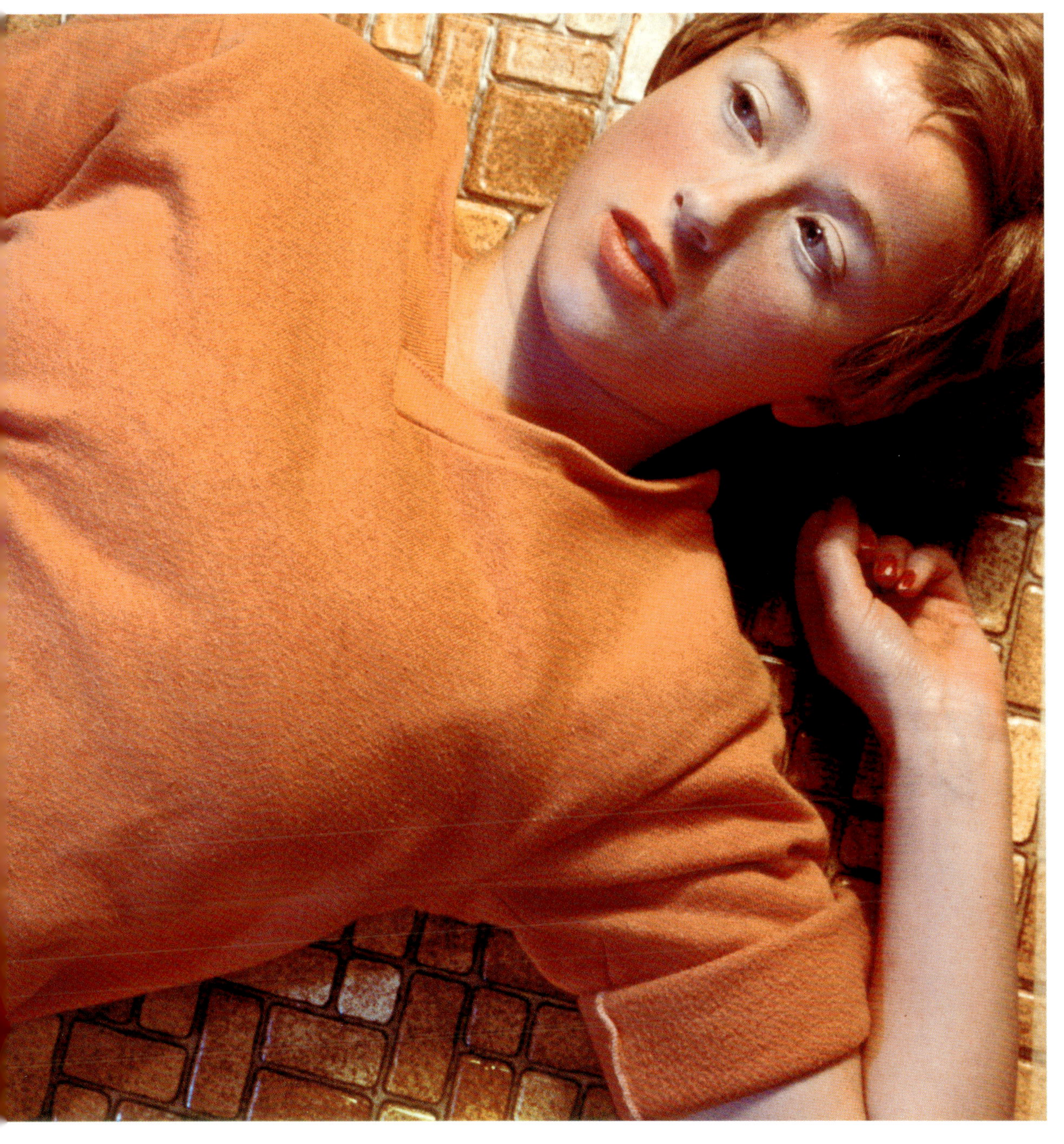

Cindy Sherman (American, born 1954). Untitled #96. 1981. Chromogenic color print, 24 × 48″ (61 × 121.9 cm).
THE MUSEUM OF MODERN ART, NEW YORK. GIFT OF CARL D. LOBELL

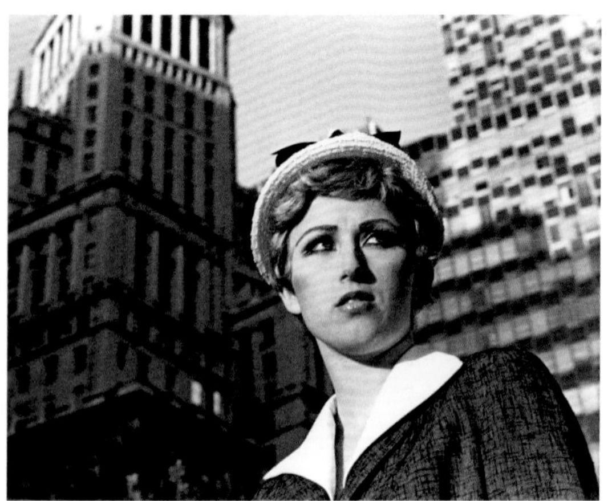

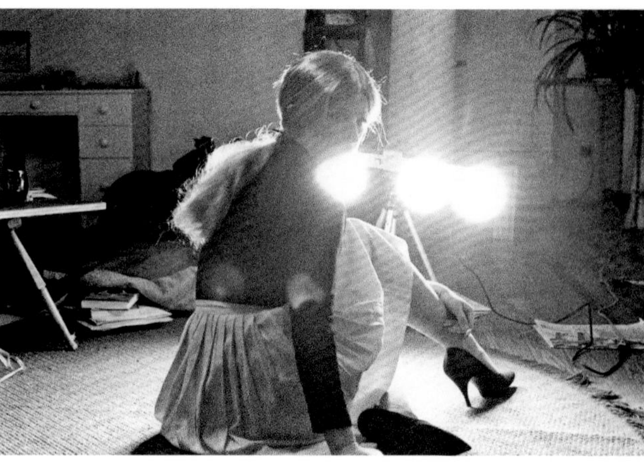

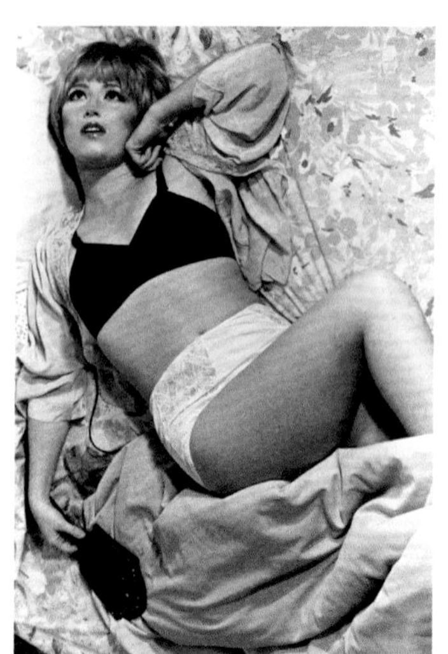

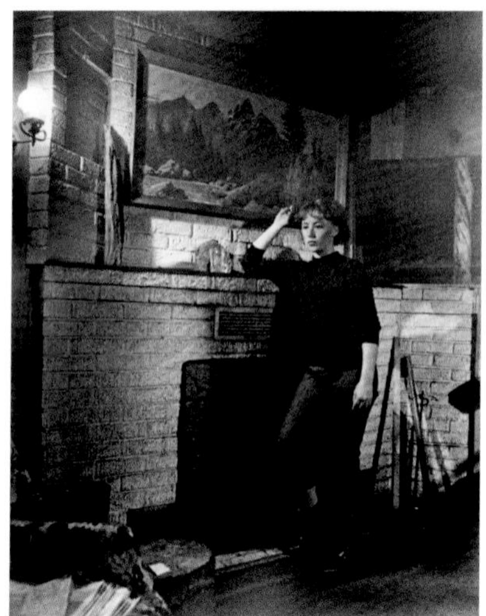

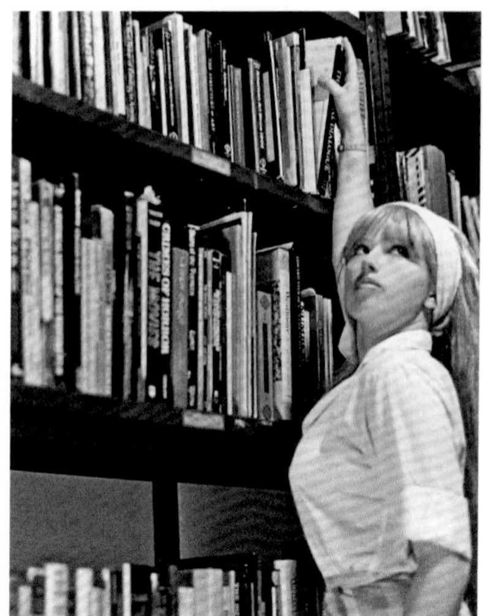

FIGS. 1–5. Clockwise from top left: Cindy Sherman (American, born 1954). Untitled Film Still #21. 1978. Gelatin silver print, 7 ½ × 9 ½" (19.1 × 24.1 cm). THE MUSEUM OF MODERN ART, NEW YORK. HORACE W. GOLDSMITH FUND THROUGH ROBERT B. MENSCHEL; Untitled Film Still #62. 1977. Gelatin silver print, 6 ¼ × 9 5⁄16" (15.9 × 23.6 cm). THE MUSEUM OF MODERN ART, NEW YORK. GIFT OF THE ARTIST; Untitled Film Still #13. 1978. Gelatin silver print, 9 7⁄16 × 7 ½" (24 × 19.1 cm). THE MUSEUM OF MODERN ART, NEW YORK. ACQUIRED THROUGH THE GENEROSITY OF JO CAROLE AND RONALD S. LAUDER IN MEMORY OF EUGENE M. SCHWARTZ; Untitled Film Still #37. 1979. Gelatin silver print, 9 7⁄16 × 7 9⁄16" (24 × 19.2 cm). THE MUSEUM OF MODERN ART, NEW YORK. PURCHASE; Untitled Film Still #6. 1977. Gelatin silver print, 9 7⁄16 × 6 ½" (24 × 16.5 cm). THE MUSEUM OF MODERN ART, NEW YORK. ACQUIRED THROUGH THE GENEROSITY OF JO CAROLE AND RONALD S. LAUDER IN MEMORY OF EUGENE M. SCHWARTZ

FOR MORE THAN FORTY YEARS CINDY SHERMAN HAS BEEN CELEBRATED FOR HER extraordinary ability to create vivid scenes and characters. She first captivated the art world with her Untitled Film Stills[1] (1977–80), a landmark series of eight-by-ten-inch black-and-white photographs in which she transforms herself into an astonishing variety of female stereotypes drawn from Hollywood and European art-house films as well as B movies **[FIGS. 1–5]**. The Stills inspired countless critics to discuss Sherman's work in relation to the medium of film, with cinematic terms—such as director, auteur, actress, makeup artist, costume designer, stylist, and lighting technician—often being used to describe the artist. Less frequently discussed, though equally important for understanding Sherman's work, is her use of print media, especially magazines. Since early in her career she has investigated the visual conventions of magazines—from pulp and confession rags to fashion and men's erotic magazines—and considered their effects on our individual and collective psyches. This book is about one of Sherman's earliest forays into the visual culture of magazines, the so-called Centerfolds series (1981)—specifically *Untitled #96*—in which she explores issues of representation, power, and gender in relationship to the pornographic centerfold.

In the early 1980s Sherman was commissioned to create new work to be published in the influential art magazine *Artforum*. She chose to take on the theme of the centerfold model. Although the magazine's editor ultimately rejected the project, the artist decided to pursue it on her own, producing a total of twelve large-scale color photographs (*Untitled #85–#96*). The Centerfolds show young, often reclining women (all are, of course, Sherman herself) in private, somewhat melancholic moments of reverie, longing, or waiting. Some simply stare into space, their expressions difficult to read. While none of the photographs are nudes or explicitly sexual, they were intended to make viewers question their conscious or unconscious assumptions and impulses when looking at a pornographic centerfold—a format that perhaps had a far greater hold on the male (and female) imagination in the 1980s than it does today, when pornography has largely migrated from print to digital platforms.

In *Untitled #96* a young woman lies on her back against a "harvest gold" brick-patterned vinyl floor of a type that was common in 1970s American kitchens. She wears a schoolgirl outfit: an orange V-neck sweater, an orange-and-white gingham skirt, and white tennis shoes. Her hair is cropped and her face bare of any obvious makeup. She clutches a scrap of newspaper that appears to have been torn from the classified section. Among the only words that can be deciphered are "know yourself/know your future," suggesting a fortune or horoscope. Her left leg is tucked under her right and bent back so that her heel touches her backside, and her skirt rides up, exposing part of her thigh. There is something unsettling about this tightly cropped figure, splayed diagonally across the horizontal picture plane, with her vacant, faraway expression. Her mood seems to change, depending on how we imagine the narrative that is simultaneously implied and withheld. Is she hopeful or wistful? Slightly apprehensive or just introspective? Her complete absorption in her own thoughts and lack of awareness of being seen gives her a vulnerability—and casts the viewer as a complicit voyeur.

When the Centerfolds debuted at the New York gallery Metro Pictures in November 1981, the photographs became a lightning rod for political debates. Some critics read them as a feminist parody of soft-core porn; others criticized them for depicting women as victims, inviting identification or even titillation. As the artist later explained, "I wanted a man opening up the magazine to suddenly look at it in expectation of something lascivious and then feel like the violator that they would be, looking at this woman who's perhaps a victim . . . [although] I didn't think of them as victims at the time."[2] The series placed Sherman's work in the spotlight, and *Untitled #96* in particular has become iconic. (Indeed, it was chosen as the cover image for the catalogue to the major traveling retrospective of Sherman's work organized by the Museum of Contemporary Art, Los Angeles, and the Museum of Contemporary Art Chicago in 1997.) Considered in the context of Sherman's career to date, the Centerfolds can be seen as a pivot point between the artist's early work with cinematic roles and genres and the many other complex subjects she has gone on to tackle.

—

Cynthia Morris Sherman was born in Glen Ridge, New Jersey, in 1954, the youngest of five children. She grew up in Huntington Beach, a Long Island suburb forty miles outside Manhattan. As a child, she loved to play dress-up, creating elaborate costumes out of a trunk of old clothes, some of which had belonged to her great-grandmother **[FIG. 6]**. She would spend hours transforming herself into various make-believe characters and creatures. "I was more interested in being different from other little girls who would dress up as princesses or fairies," Sherman recalled. "I would be the ugly old witch or the monster."[3]

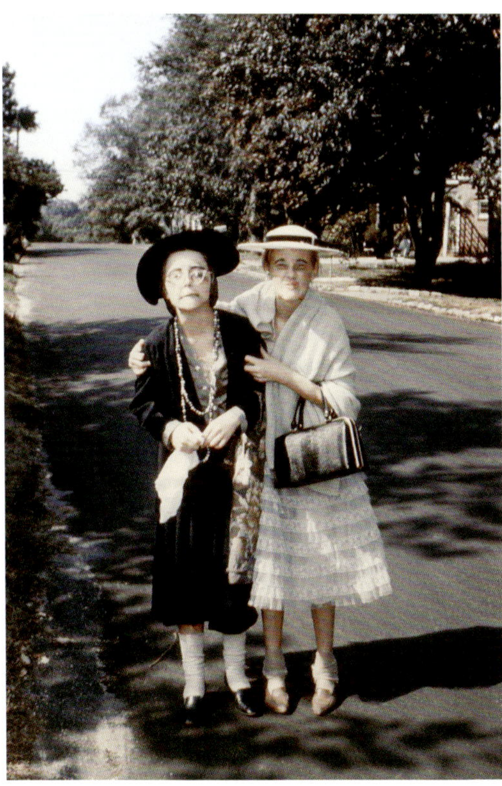

FIG. 6. Snapshot of Cindy Sherman (left) and friend Janet Zink dressed up as old ladies, c. 1966

Coming of age at a time when more and more American families owned television sets, she also watched a lot of movies on TV. In 1972 she enrolled at Buffalo State College in western New York, where she majored in art and famously flunked a required introductory photography course because of her undeveloped technical abilities. It was while taking the class again with a different instructor, who taught Sherman about more conceptual modes of working, that the artist began to take pictures of herself. Around the same time, she started dating fellow student Robert Longo. Together with a group of other young artists, they founded the alternative space Hallwalls in Buffalo, staging exhibitions of each other's work and organizing workshops and lectures with distinguished contemporary artists such as Robert Irwin and Vito Acconci.

During this period, Sherman experimented with altering her appearance using wigs, makeup, glasses, and clothing, and by varying her facial expressions and body language. She documented these dramatic makeovers and exhibited the resulting photographs in a serial manner to suggest the passage of time. For example, in *Untitled #479*, made for a class assignment, she metamorphizes over the course of twenty-three images from an ordinary, bookish college student into a glamorous, cigarette-smoking vamp **[FIG. 7]** Sherman's experiments

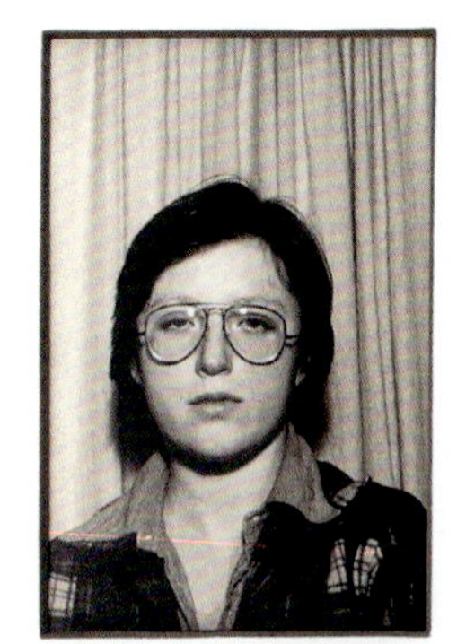
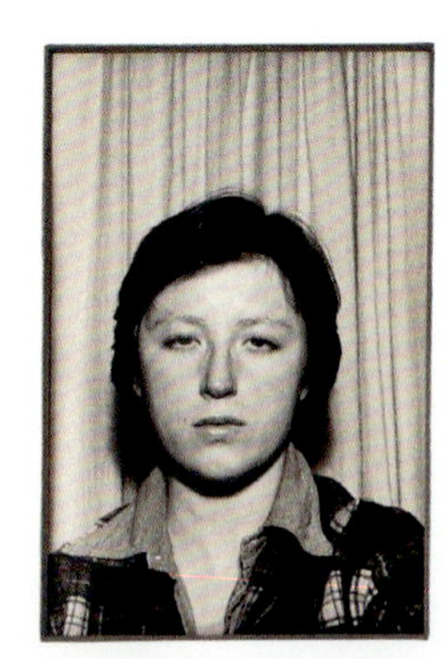
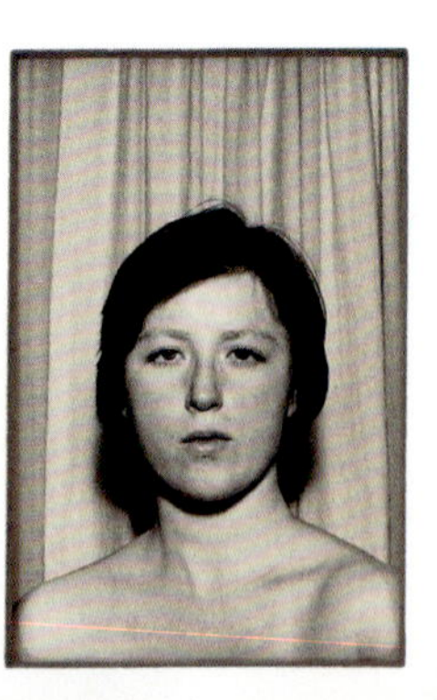
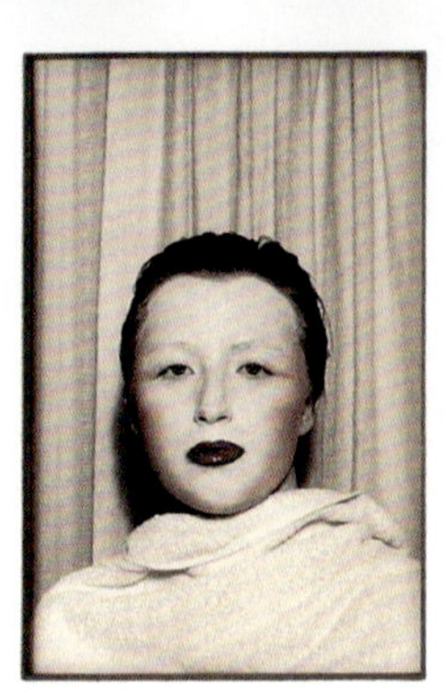
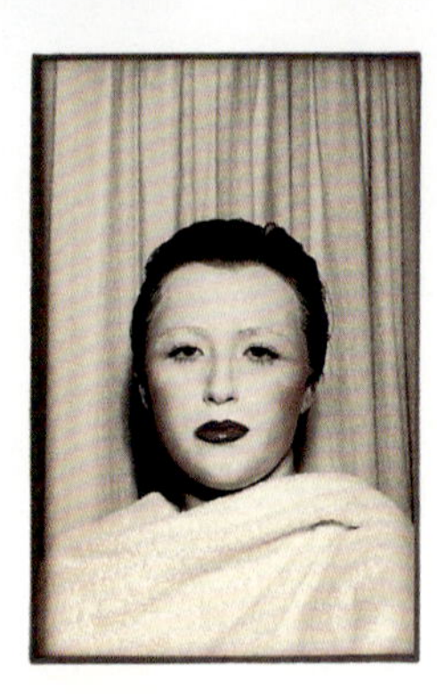
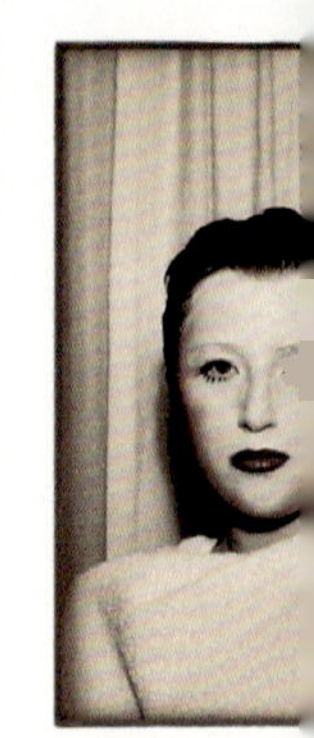
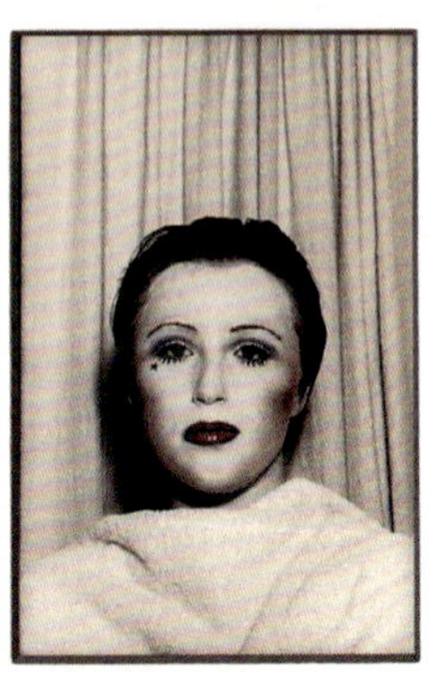
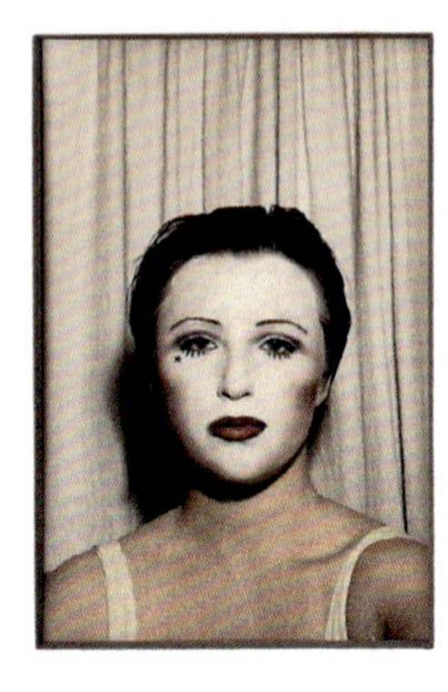
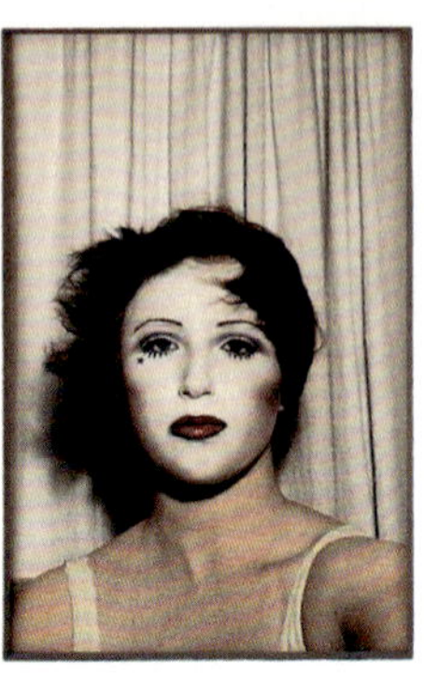

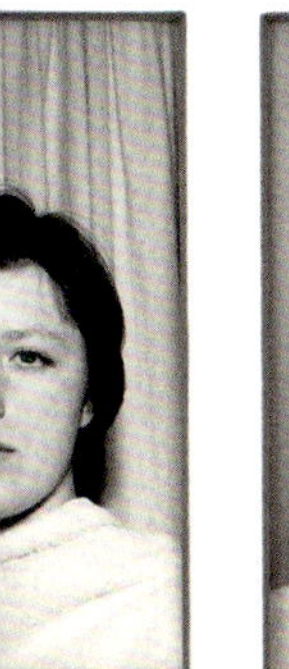
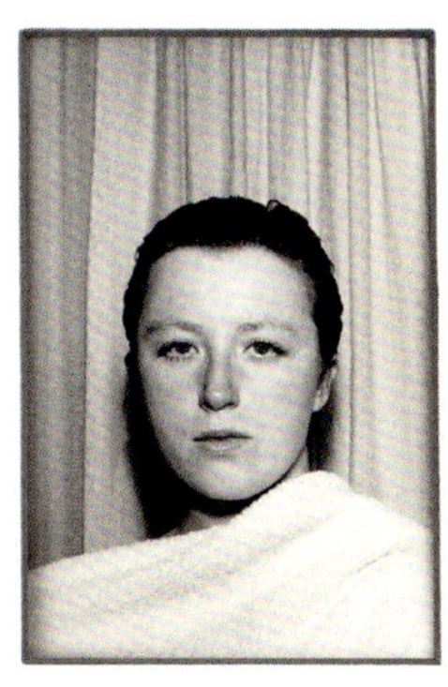
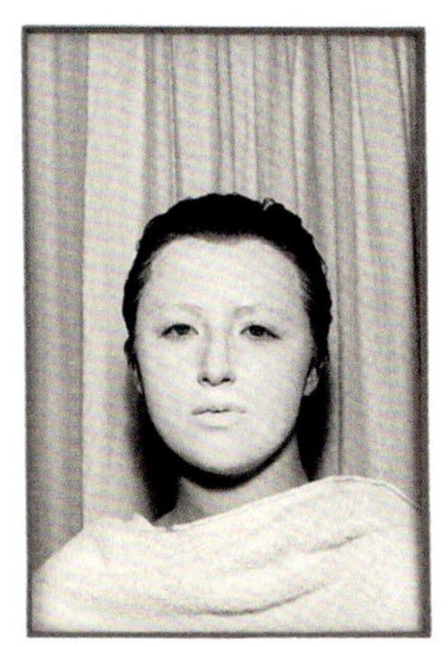
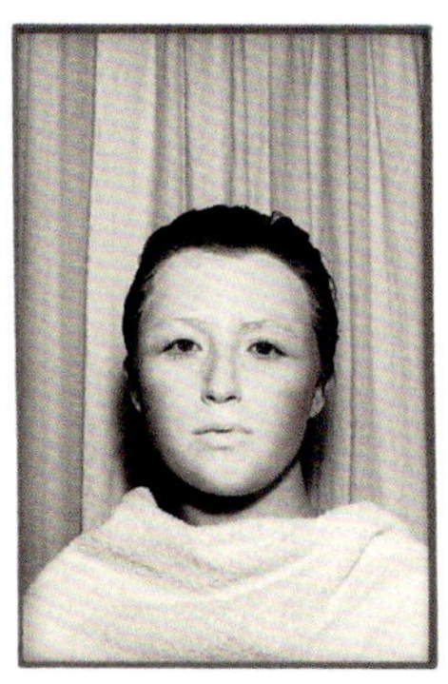
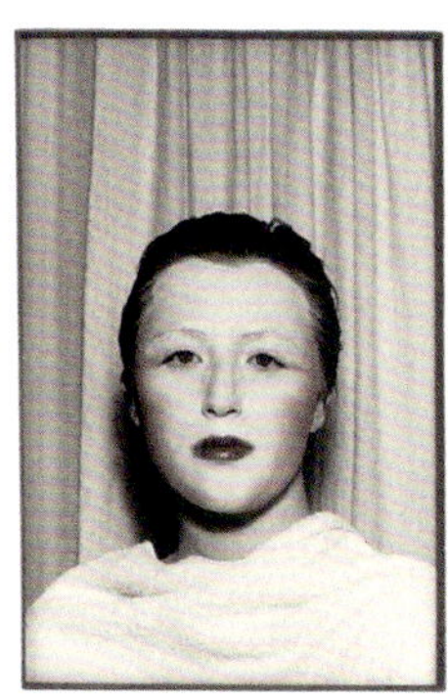
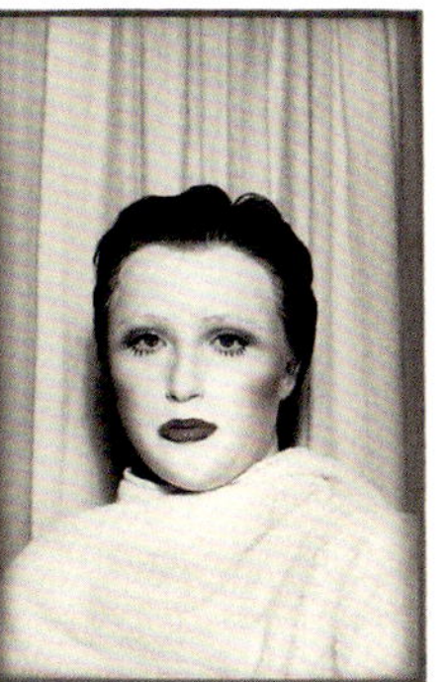
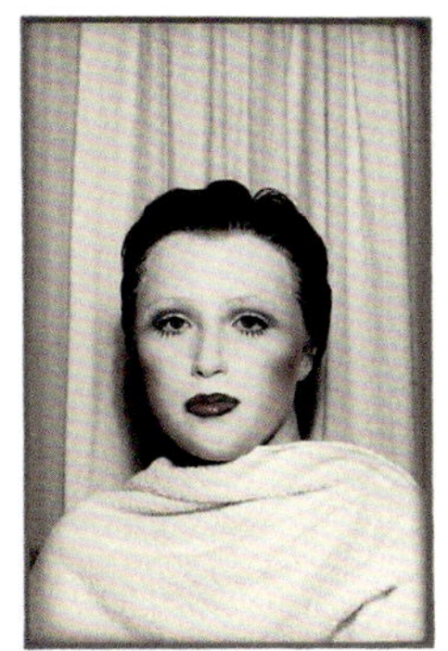
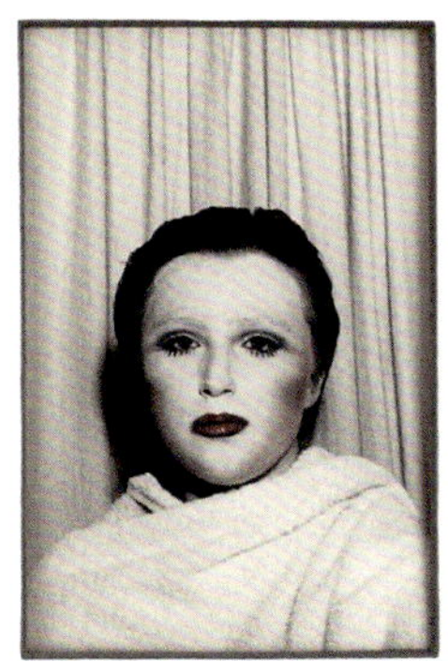
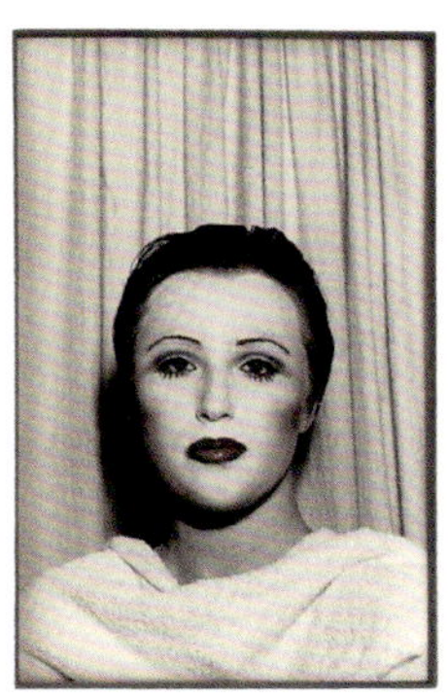
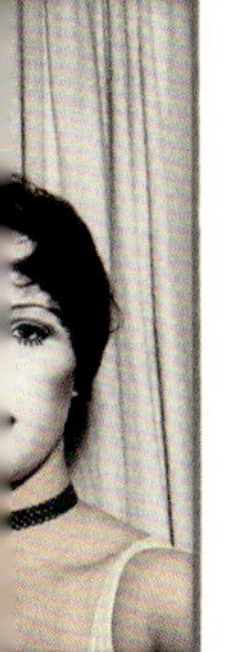
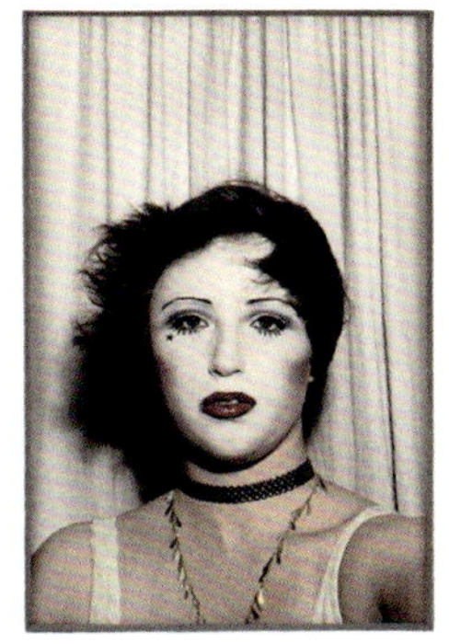
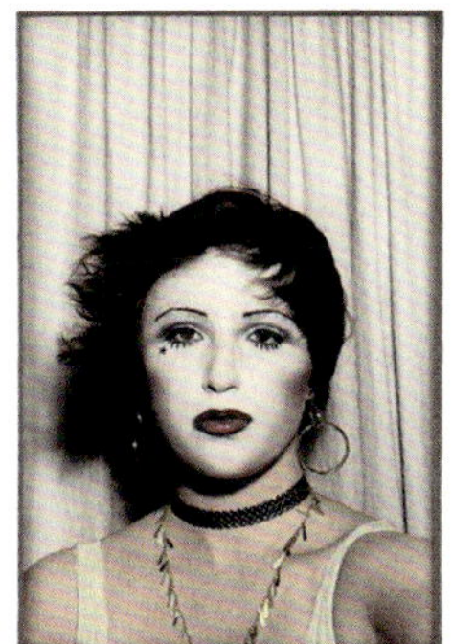
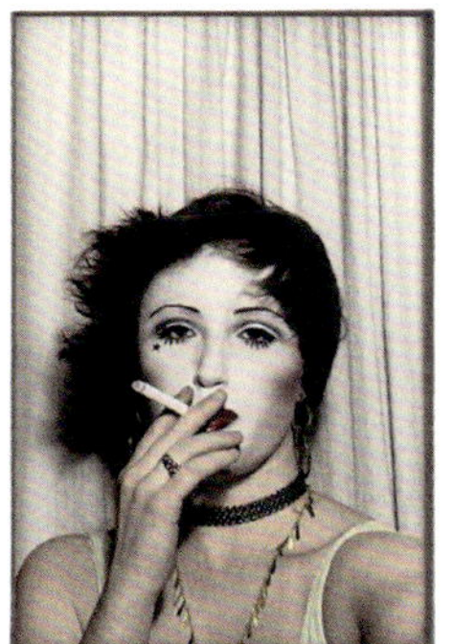
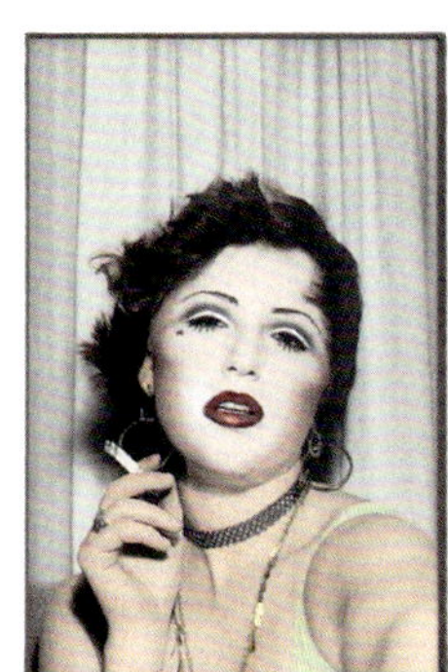

FIG. 7. Cindy Sherman (American, born 1954). Untitled #479. 1975. Twenty-three hand-colored gelatin silver prints, overall 20 ½ × 33 ½" (52.1 × 85.1 cm). COLLECTION DOROTHY AND PETER WALDT

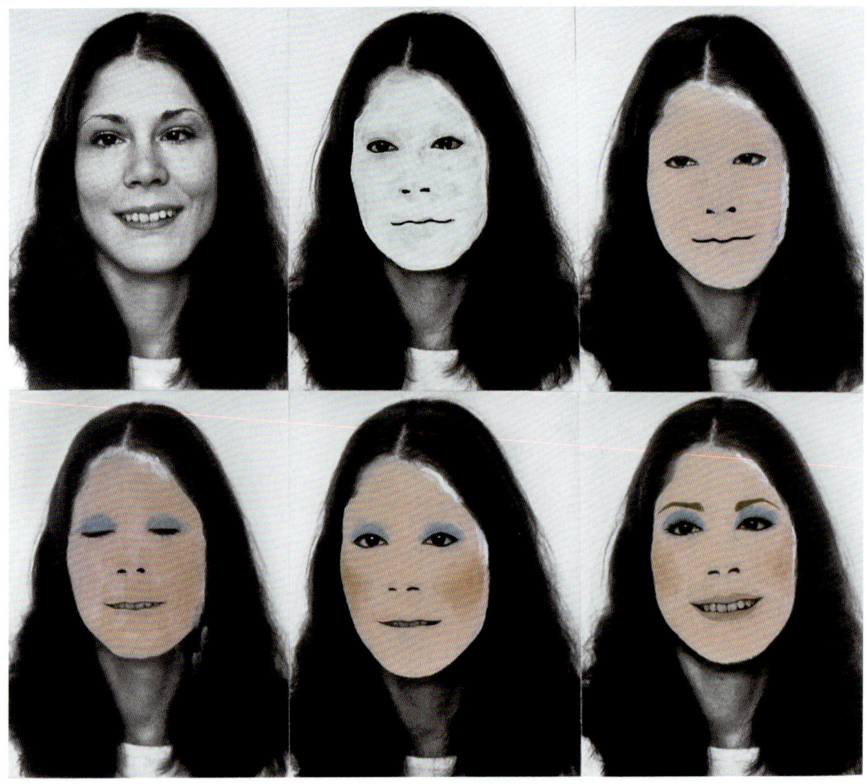

FIG. 8. Suzy Lake (Canadian, born United States 1947). *A Genuine Simulation of . . . No. 2*. 1973–74. Six gelatin silver prints and commercial makeup mounted on fiber-based print, 27 9⁄16 × 32 ½" (70 × 82.5 cm). THE MONTREAL MUSEUM OF FINE ARTS. SAIDYE AND SAMUEL BRONFMAN COLLECTION OF CANADIAN ART

with self-transformation were influenced by an earlier generation of performance and Conceptual artists such as Suzy Lake [**FIG. 8**], Eleanor Antin, and Hannah Wilke [**FIG. 9**], all of whom used serialized self-portraits to engage issues of gender and identity. Sherman also turned to magazines as a source of inspiration during college. In a series of works called the Cover Girls, she parodied covers from women's and fashion magazines, including *Vogue*, *Cosmopolitan*, *Redbook*, and *Family Circle* [**FIGS. 10, 11**]. She displayed the original magazine covers alongside mock-ups in which her face is superimposed on the cover model's, first striking an uncanny resemblance to the original and then spoofing the image with a goofy or unflattering expression. Demonstrating Sherman's impressive skill in mimicry, the series was an early take on subjects the artist would return to again and again later in her career: the grotesque and women in the media.

After college, Sherman moved with Longo to Manhattan, where they fell in with a group of artists that would later become known as the Pictures Generation,

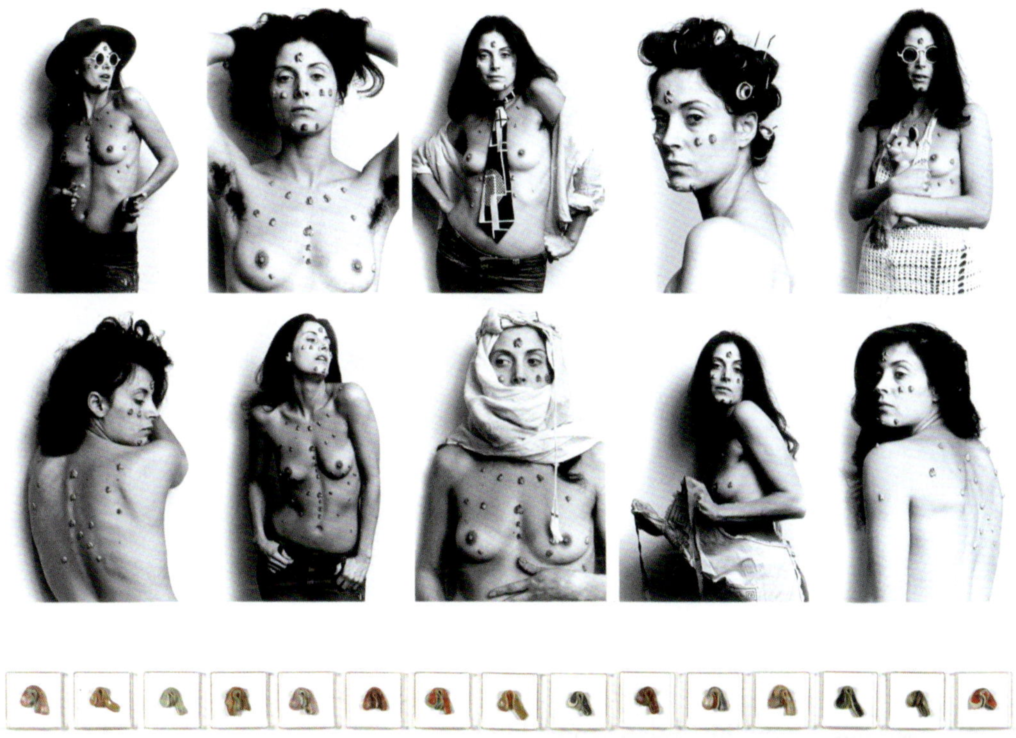

FIG. 9. Hannah Wilke (American, 1940–1993). *S.O.S.—Starification Object Series*. 1974–82. Ten gelatin silver prints with chewing gum sculptures, overall 40 × 58 ½ × 2 ¼" (101.6 × 148.6 × 5.7 cm). THE MUSEUM OF MODERN ART, NEW YORK. PURCHASE

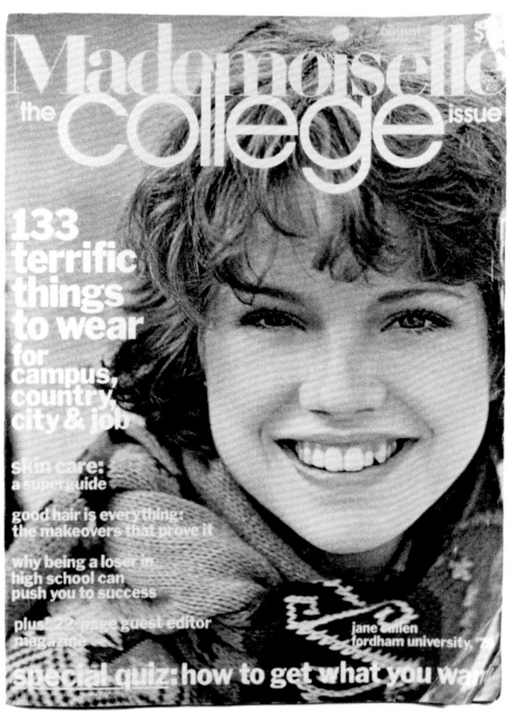

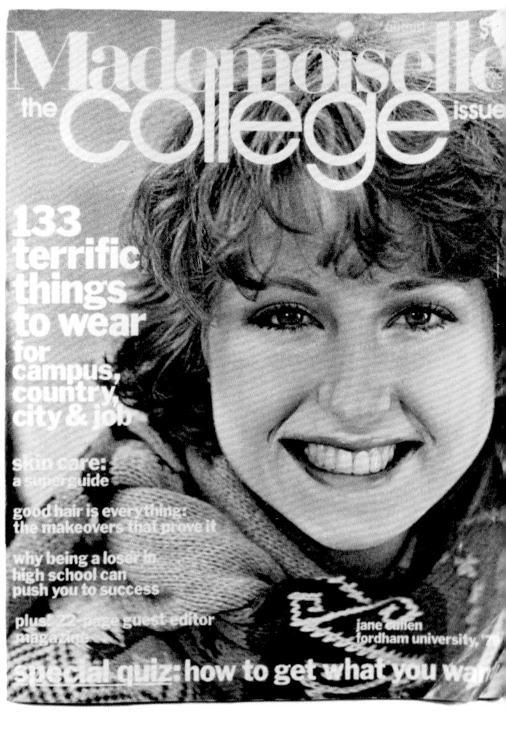

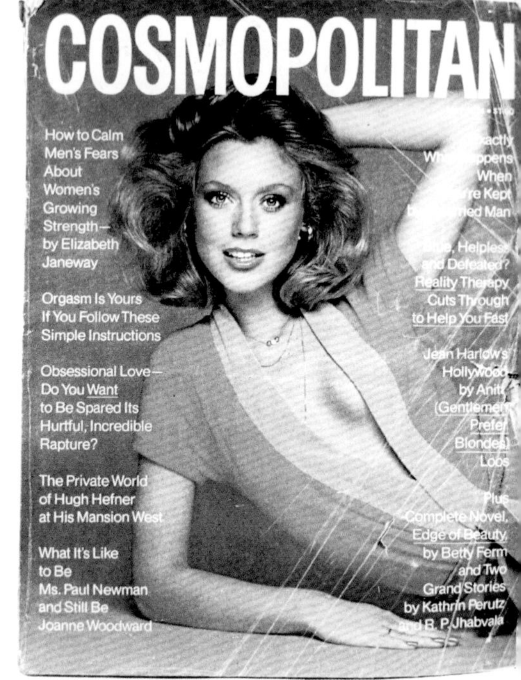

FIG. 10. Cindy Sherman (American, born 1954). *Cover Girl (Mademoiselle)*. 1975/2011. Three gelatin silver prints, each 10 ½ × 8" (26.7 × 20.3 cm)

FIG. 11. Cindy Sherman (American, born 1954). *Cover Girl (Cosmopolitan)*. 1975/2011. Three gelatin silver prints, each 10 ½ × 8" (26.7 × 20.3 cm)

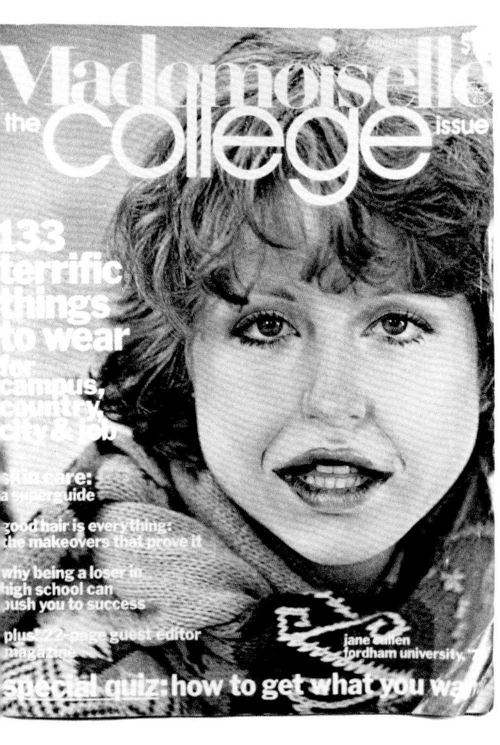

Mademoiselle
the College issue
133 terrific things to wear for campus, country, city & job
skin care: a superguide
good hair is everything: the makeovers that prove it
why being a loser in high school can push you to success
plus: 22-page guest editor magazine
jane cullen fordham university
special quiz: how to get what you

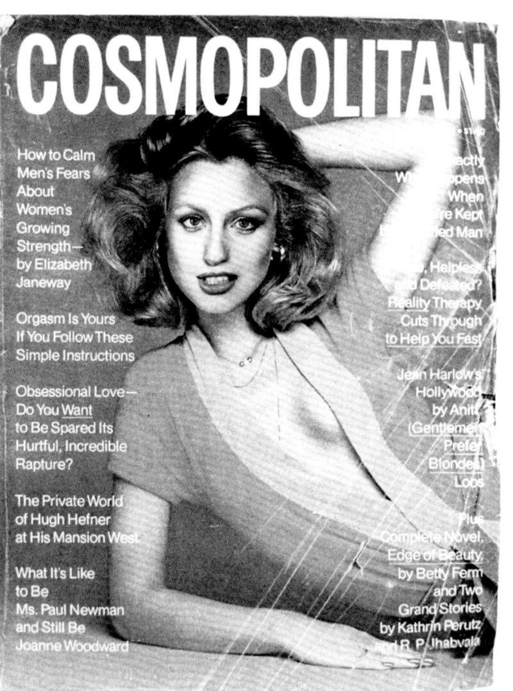

COSMOPOLITAN
How to Calm Men's Fears About Women's Growing Strength—by Elizabeth Janeway
Orgasm Is Yours If You Follow These Simple Instructions
Obsessional Love—Do You Want to Be Spared Its Hurtful, Incredible Rapture?
The Private World of Hugh Hefner at His Mansion West
What It's Like to Be Ms. Paul Newman and Still Be Joanne Woodward
and Defeated? Reality Therapy Cuts Through to Help You Fast
Jean Harlow's Hollywood
(Gentlemen Prefer Blondes) Loos
Plus Complete Novel, Edge of Beauty, by Betty Ferm and Two Grand Stories by Kathrin Perutz and R. P. Jhabvala

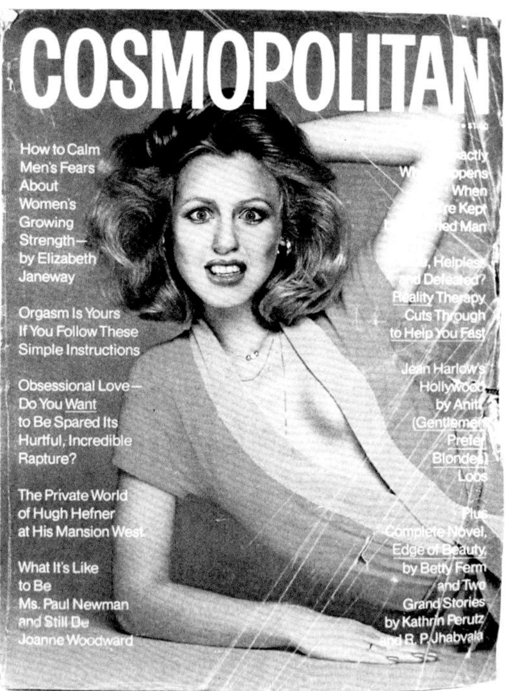

COSMOPOLITAN
How to Calm Men's Fears About Women's Growing Strength—by Elizabeth Janeway
Orgasm Is Yours If You Follow These Simple Instructions
Obsessional Love—Do You Want to Be Spared Its Hurtful, Incredible Rapture?
The Private World of Hugh Hefner at His Mansion West
What It's Like to Be Ms. Paul Newman and Still Be Joanne Woodward
and Defeated? Reality Therapy Cuts Through to Help You Fast
Jean Harlow's Hollywood
(Gentlemen Prefer Blondes) Loos
Plus Complete Novel, Edge of Beauty, by Betty Ferm and Two Grand Stories by Kathrin Perutz and R. P. Jhabvala

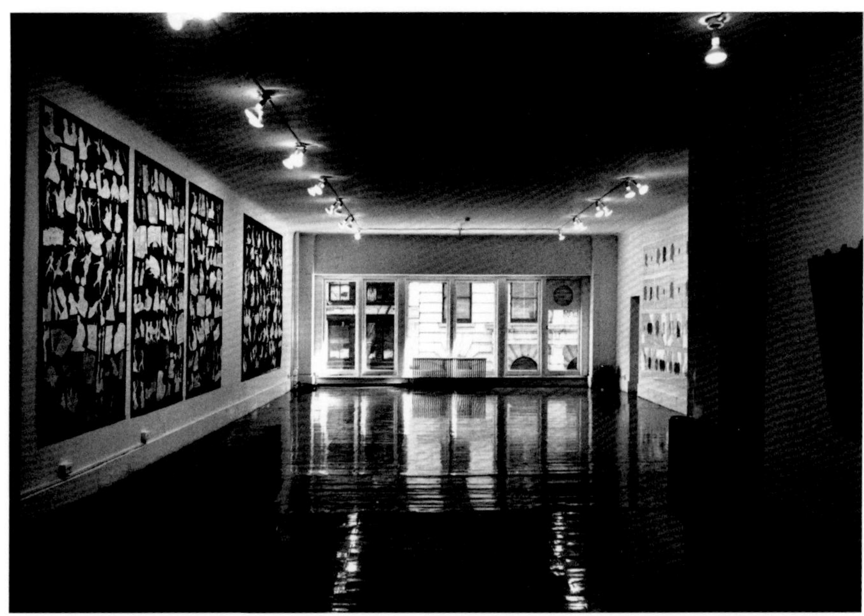

FIG. 12. Installation view of *Pictures*, Artists Space, New York, September 24–October 29, 1977. Photo: D. James Dee

so named after the landmark 1977 *Pictures* exhibition curated by art historian Douglas Crimp at Artists Space in New York **[FIG. 12]**. Many artists of the Pictures Generation—which included Sherrie Levine, Richard Prince, Barbara Kruger, Troy Brauntuch, Jack Goldstein, and Louise Lawler, among others—drew on and subverted the pervasive visual culture of mass media as a way of revealing its implicit, structural biases. As Crimp wrote in his catalogue essay for *Pictures*: "To an ever greater extent our experience is governed by pictures, pictures in newspapers and magazines, on television and in the cinema. Next to these pictures firsthand experience begins to retreat, to seem more and more trivial. While it once seemed that pictures had the function of interpreting reality, it now seems that they have usurped it."[4] This new generation of artists, he argued, approached this situation critically, making works that sought to expose the ways in which images convey meaning and communicate messages. To do so, they commonly deployed the strategy of appropriation: the intentional borrowing, copying, and alteration of existing images. Two iconic series exemplifying this tactic are Prince's Untitled (Cowboy) (1989; **FIG. 13**), for which he photographed cigarette ads from magazines, leaving out any branding or text, and Levine's Untitled, After Walker Evans (1981; **FIG. 14**), for which she photographed reproductions of the titular artist's Depression-era work. In this manner the Pictures artists not only shed light on American values and culture but also challenged notions of originality and artistic genius that had been championed by early-twentieth-century modernists—

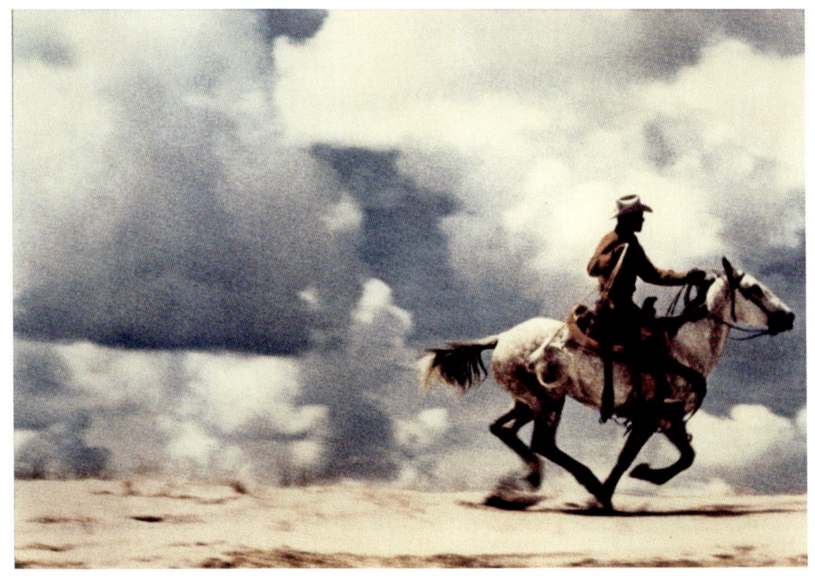

FIG. 13. Richard Prince (American, born 1949). *Untitled (Cowboy)*. 1989. Chromogenic color print, 50 × 70" (127 × 177.8 cm)

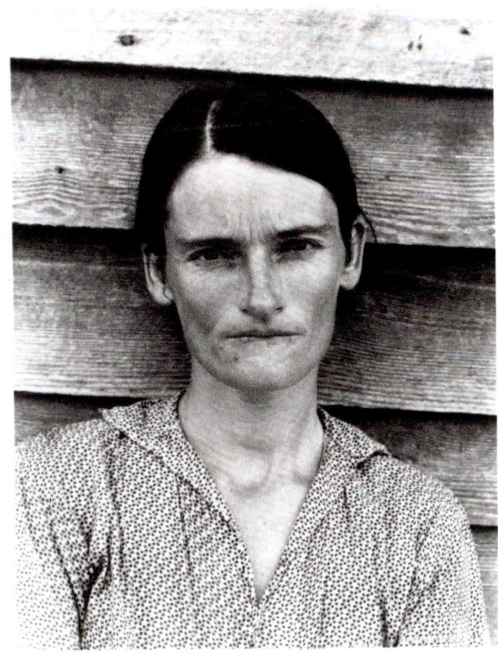

FIG. 14. Sherrie Levine (American, born 1947). *After Walker Evans: 4*. 1981. Gelatin silver print, 5 1⁄16 × 3 7⁄8" (12.8 × 9.8 cm). THE METROPOLITAN MUSEUM OF ART, NEW YORK. GIFT OF THE ARTIST

ushering in a new era that theorists termed *post*modernism. Though Sherman was not in fact included in the original *Pictures* exhibition, when Crimp published a revised version of his essay in the arts journal *October* in 1979, he discussed her Untitled Film Stills at length, retroactively solidifying her primary and influential position among these artists.

The Stills grew out of Sherman's habit—stemming from childhood but becoming more sophisticated and nuanced in college—of dressing up as various characters, sometimes publicly. She would nonchalantly appear at parties or openings posing as a pregnant woman or Lucille Ball, or show up at her day job as a receptionist at Artists Space dressed as a nurse or 1950s secretary. Sherman soon began to photograph herself in costume, using a cable shutter release or occasionally asking someone else to take the picture. In the Stills, she inhabited various female "roles," many of which appear to have been drawn from classic Hollywood cinema, such as ingenue, femme fatale, and career girl. The images—seventy in all—imitate the publicity stills once commonly distributed in movie press kits: throwaway eight-by-ten-inch black-and-white photographs **[FIG. 15]**. "I wanted them to seem cheap and trashy," Sherman recalled, "[like] something you'd find in a novelty store and buy for a quarter. I didn't want them to look like art."[5]

So evocative were they of stereotypes found in popular cinema that some viewers mistakenly thought the Untitled Film Stills referenced actual movies—attesting to the images' success at tapping into our collective cultural memory. As the art historian Craig Owens described, "Sherman's women are not women but images of women, specular models of femininity projected by the media to encourage imitation, identification; they are, in other words, tropes, figures."[6] This quality of appearing familiar yet untraceable to a particular source made Sherman's work well-disposed to postmodernist readings. For example, Rosalind Krauss drew on the French sociologist Jean Baudrillard's theory of the simulacrum—in which he argued that mass media has completely replaced reality with free-floating signs and images—to interpret Sherman's photographs. Krauss claimed that "the condition of Sherman's work in the *Stills*—and part of their point, we could say—is the simulacral nature of what they contain, its condition of being a copy *without* an original."[7] Others noted the way her photographs deviate from traditional self-portraiture in a manner that undermines modernist notions of truth, authorship, originality, and authenticity. "[Sherman's] photographs reverse the terms of art and autobiography," Crimp wrote a few years after *Pictures*. "They use art not to reveal the artist's true self but to show the self as an imaginary construct. There is no real Cindy Sherman in these photographs; there are only the guises she assumes. And she does not create these guises; she simply chooses them in the way that any of us do."[8]

A number of other critics have read Sherman's early work through a feminist lens. In an influential 1983 text for *Screen* magazine, Judith Williamson argued that

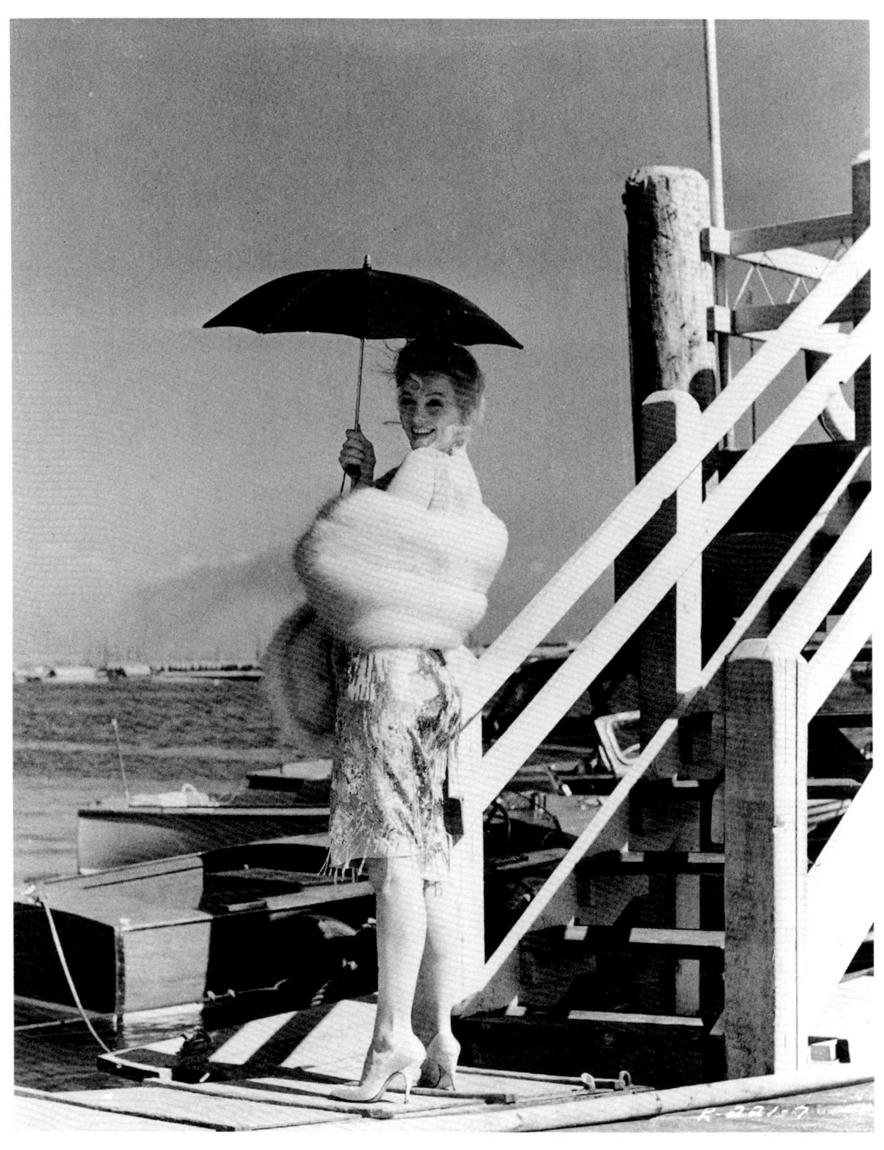

FIG. 15. Publicity still for Billy Wilder's *Some Like It Hot* (1959). Marilyn Monroe

Sherman lays bare how the "imagery and experience of femininity" are shaped by representations of women in "films, news photos, advertisements, and media generally."[9] The artist does so "by presenting a whole lexicon of feminine identities" drawn from mass culture, "all of them played by 'her'"—such as "femme fatale," "nice girl," and "dumb blonde," among other stock examples.[10] Williamson further contends that Sherman's images show "not just a range of feminine expressions . . . but the *process* of the 'feminine' as an effect."[11] This debunking of the supposed innocence of media depictions of women resonates with the theory of the male gaze developed by the film theorist Laura Mulvey. In her 1973 essay "Visual Pleasure and Narrative Cinema," Mulvey analyzed the ways in which Hollywood cinema posits female characters as passive objects to be looked at, while conflating the gazes of the camera and viewer with straight male desire. Like these mainstream movies, Sherman's photographs largely focus on white, heterosexual experiences of identity; yet because the artist locates gender identity within cultural and visual representations, she demonstrates that gender is not intrinsic to the body. Thus her work is not incompatible with, and in some ways has helped pave the way for, more complicated understandings of gender as something that isn't essential to or fixed in our nature but rooted in artifice, masquerade, and performance.

Just as she disrupts the illusion of femininity as something natural, exposing its contrived, even *constructed* nature, so Sherman also challenges the supposed transparency of photography itself—its status as a neutral "window" merely presenting reality. Instead, she underscores the narrative dimension of photography through visually complex works that allow for multiple interpretations. Sherman helped usher in a new kind of photography, a postmodern one that rejected the formalist approach of modernist photographers, who had secured the medium's recognition as a high-art form in the early twentieth century by emphasizing the qualities unique to photography while highlighting the formal properties of an image, such as tonality and composition **[FIG. 16]**. Further departing from this tradition, Sherman identifies not as a photographer but as an artist who uses photography. "I thought of my work as art, but not 'high' art," she explained. "Which was fine, because I didn't want to make anything too precious. . . . I wanted to find something that anyone could relate to without knowing about contemporary art. I wasn't thinking in terms of precious prints or archival quality. . . . The issue still wasn't the quality of the print, it was about the idea."[12]

In 1980 Sherman joined the roster at the newly minted Metro Pictures, the gallery that, arguably more than any other, put the Pictures Generation on the map of the art world establishment. (Her first solo show there debuted a series of large color photographs known as the Rear Screen Projections [1980–81], which feature actress-types similar to those in the Untitled Film Stills. The figures are posed against outdoor backgrounds that were projected on a screen in

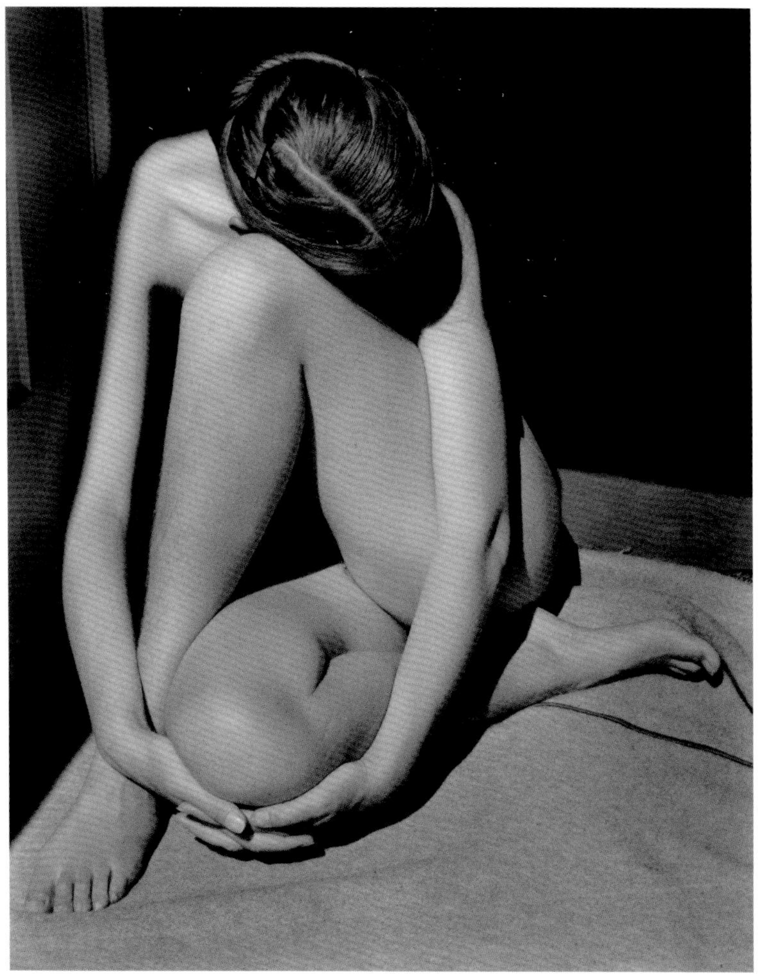

FIG. 16. Edward Weston (American, 1886–1958). *Nude.* 1936. Gelatin silver print, printed 1952, 9 ½ × 7 9⁄16" (24.1 × 19.3 cm). THE MUSEUM OF MODERN ART, NEW YORK. GIFT OF T.J. MALONY

Sherman's studio, riffing on the old-school Hollywood special effect after which the series is named **[FIG. 17]**.) Yet even as she gained critical and commercial success, Sherman dedicated herself to modes of display and distribution outside the gallery system. Her work for and about magazines would prove central to this commitment.

—

In 1981 Sherman was commissioned by *Artforum*'s then editor in chief, Ingrid Sischy, to create a special project for a forthcoming issue. The practice of using the magazine page as a medium for art first gained prominence in the 1960s and

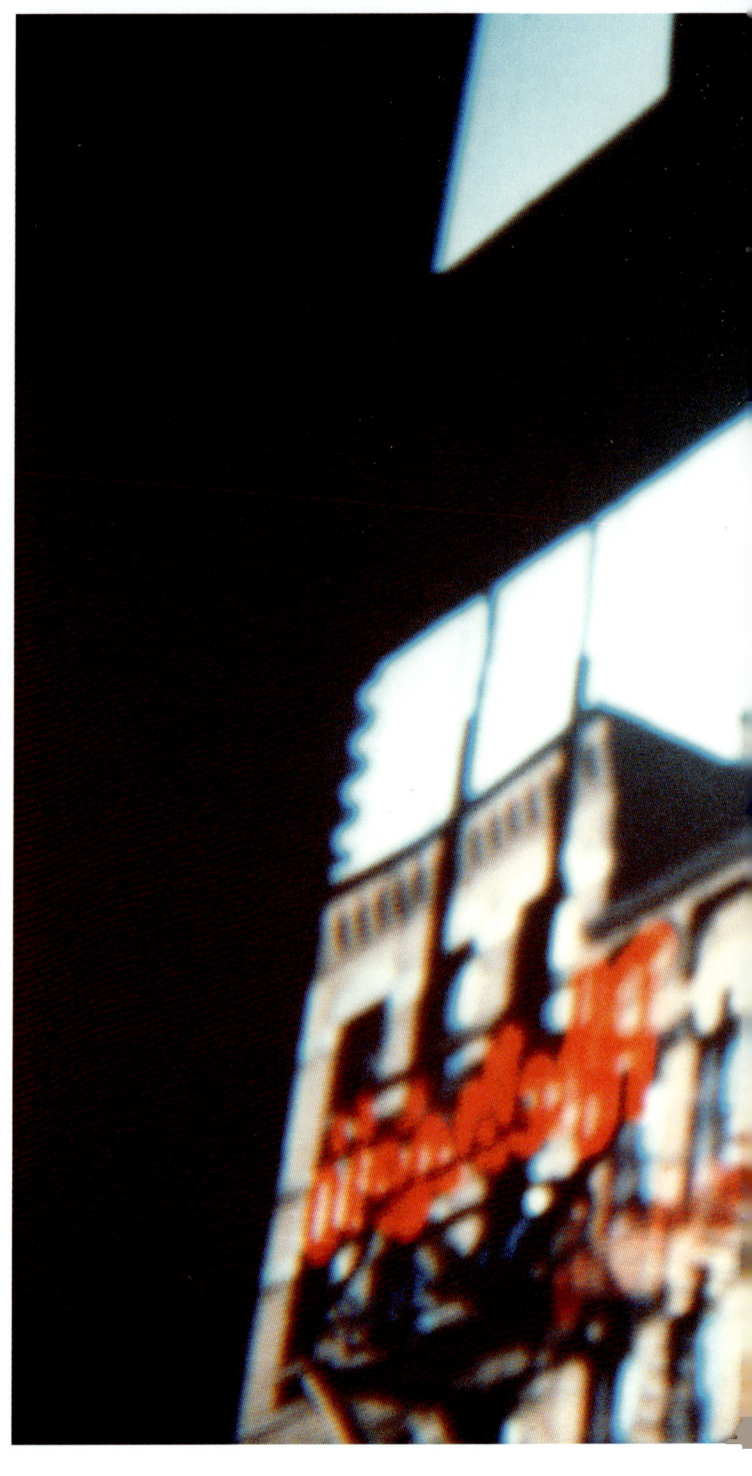

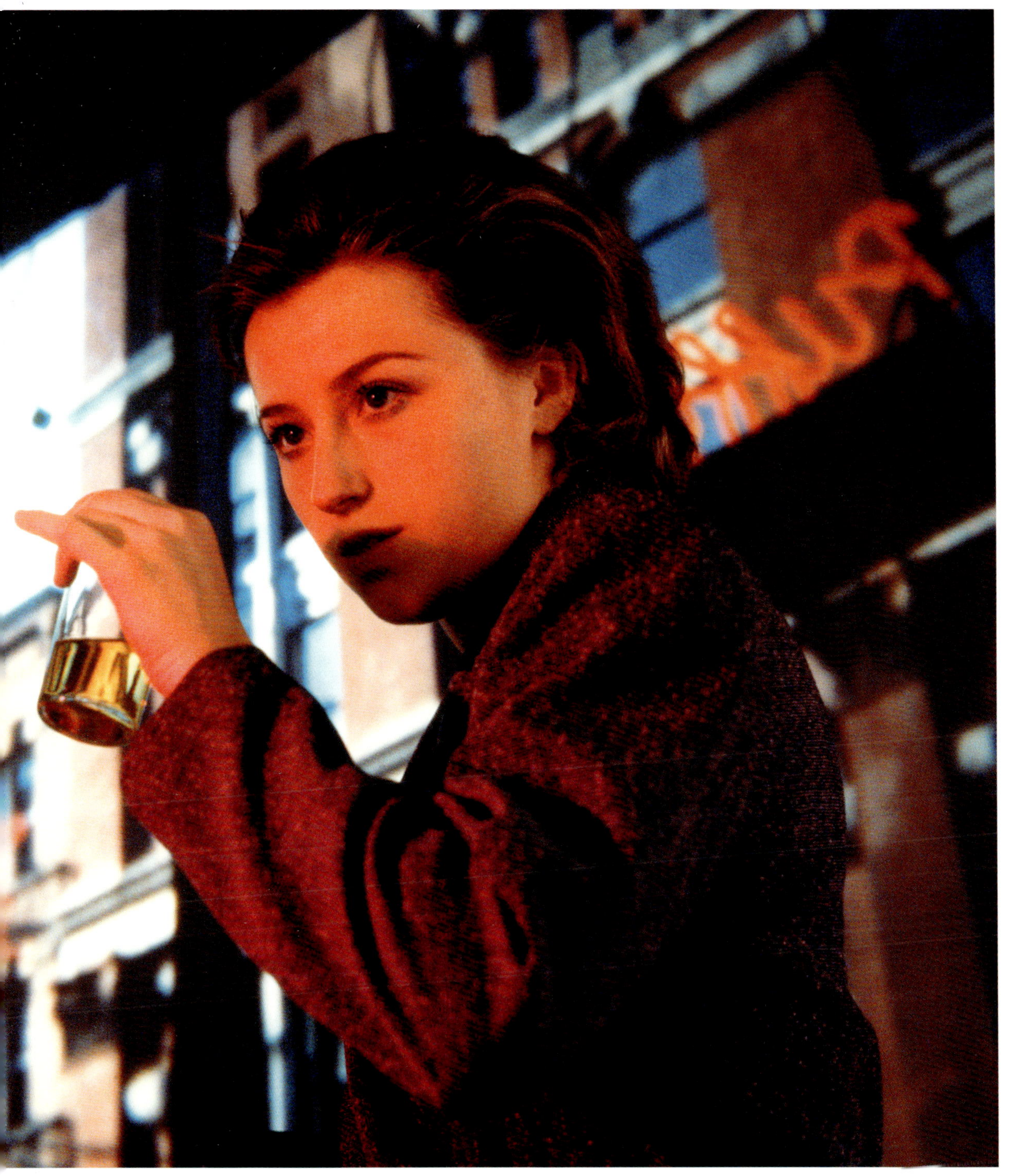

FIG. 17. Cindy Sherman (American, born 1954). Untitled #70. 1980. Chromogenic color print, 16 × 23 15/16" (40.7 × 60.8 cm). THE MUSEUM OF MODERN ART, NEW YORK. ACQUIRED THROUGH THE GENEROSITY OF JANELLE REIRING AND HELENE WINER, BY EXCHANGE

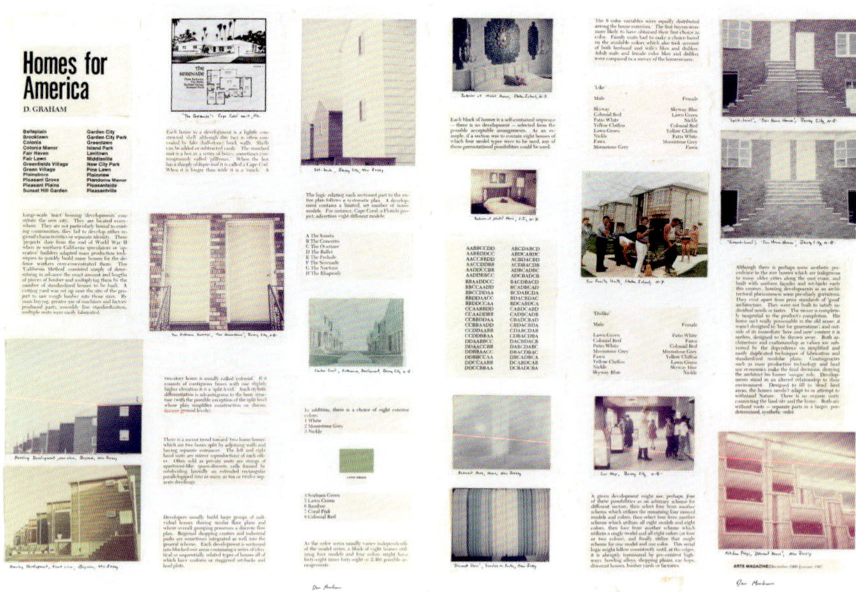

Homes for America

D. GRAHAM

Belleplain
Brooklawn
Colonia
Colonia Manor
Fair Haven
Fair Lawn
Greenfields Village
Green Village
Plainsboro
Pleasant Grove
Pleasant Plains
Sunset Hill Garden

Garden City
Garden City Park
Greenlawn
Island Park
Levittown
Middleville
New City Park
Pine Lawn
Plainview
Plandome Manor
Pleasantside
Pleasantville

FIG. 18. Dan Graham (American, born 1942). *Homes for America*. 1966–67. Gelatin silver and chromogenic color prints, paint chip, felt-tip pen, and colored pencil on two boards, each 39 15⁄16 × 33 1⁄4" (101.4 × 84.5 cm). THE MUSEUM OF MODERN ART, NEW YORK. GIFT OF HERMAN J. DALED

'70s, when Conceptual artists had turned to books and magazines as a more wide-reaching alternative to galleries. Initially, many of these published works were unannounced interventions that were intended to catch readers off guard and to upend the conventions and commercial apparatuses of print media. For example, Dan Graham's *Homes for America*, which documents suburban houses in New Jersey, appeared to be an ordinary article in a 1966–67 issue of *Arts Magazine* but functioned as sly satire: "*Esquire* magazine used to have articles about how alienating the suburbs were by sociologists, and then a . . . very well-known photographer would take glossy photographs. . . . And what I was trying to do was actually parody the whole idea," Graham explained **[FIG. 18]**.[13] Another important precedent for Sherman's Centerfolds was Adrian Piper's placement of a series of anonymous advertisements in the *Village Voice* to document and publicize her *Mythic Being* performances of the 1970s. During these performances, Piper dressed up as a man and walked the streets of New York and Cambridge, Massachusetts, gauging the reactions of passersby and observing how her own experience of racism and sexism shifted while occupying a male persona. Other artists contributed writings and projects to self-published artists' magazines such as *Aspen*, *Avalanche*, *Art-Rite*, and *Real Life*. Sischy, who was just twenty-seven years old when she took over as editor at *Artforum* in 1979, enthusiastically supported such practices, having previously worked as the director of Printed Matter, a nonprofit store in New York specializing in artists' books. In the editor's letter introducing her first issue, Sischy expressed her commitment to the "possibility of the page as a direct and primary arena, as an alternative to the wall."[14] Her invitation to Sherman to contribute an artist's project was thus part of a larger editorial program that aimed to breathe new life into the magazine and helped establish a trend that continues in *Artforum* and other magazines to this day whereby artists are invited to create works of art expressly for the page.

Given a two-page spread to work with, Sherman chose to address the centerfold photographs that were a hallmark of men's soft-core porn magazines such as *Playboy*. She ultimately created several large-scale horizontal images, each measuring two feet by four feet, in which she appears as various young female personas lying or sitting on the floor or on a sofa, crouching, or huddling into themselves. Many of the women have absent, forlorn expressions, as if they're bored or waiting for something or someone. Occasionally, they appear anxious or even scared, as in *Untitled #92*, in which a woman looks like an animal caught in headlights **[FIG. 19]**. While all of the women are fully dressed, there is often something slightly disheveled about their appearance, sometimes verging on the indecent: wet or messy hair, flushed faces moist with beads of perspiration, rumpled clothing, ridden-up tops revealing a bare midriff or a glimpse of underwear. One drenched, scantily clad figure (*Untitled #86*) lies on her side with an impassive expression, looking cold and uncomfortable, as though she'd participated in a wet T-shirt contest gone awry **[FIG. 20]**. The women seem neither fully aware nor entirely in control of the sexually suggestive nature of their poses and circumstances, giving the images a somewhat sordid, Peeping Tom quality.

Just as she had done in the Untitled Film Stills, Sherman completely transformed herself using makeup, wigs, and clothing, so that she seems to actually *become* different people. When the photos are shown in exhibition settings, the monumental scale of the prints fully immerses the viewer, adding to the pictures' emotional impact.[15] Many are haunted by a sense of foreboding, which is heightened by the tight cropping of the images so that the figures feel boxed-in by the edges of the photograph. The dramatic high-contrast lighting (an effect that Sherman produced with the help of color gels) also contributes to the various moods conveyed by these photos, suggesting twilight or evoking the glow of a fireplace or television set. Props—such as the classified ad in *Untitled #96*, the telephone in *Untitled #90* **[FIG. 21]**, and what appears to be an engagement ring in *Untitled #89* **[FIG. 22]**—hint at vague, unspecified narratives. One critic compared the women in these photographs to the heroines in confession magazines such as *Modern Romances* and *True Confessions,* which first became popular in the 1920s, marketing melodramatic first-person accounts by female narrators

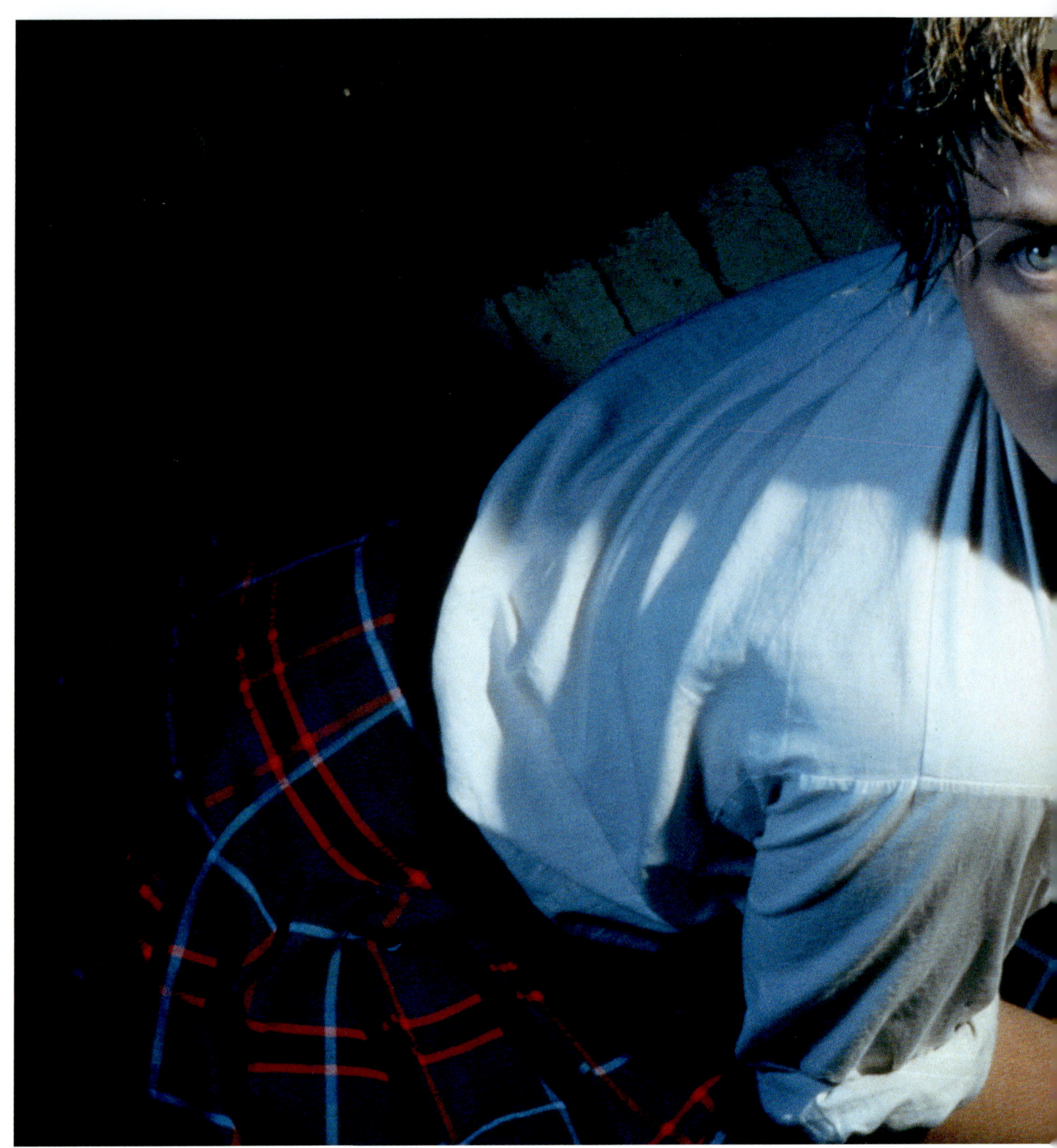

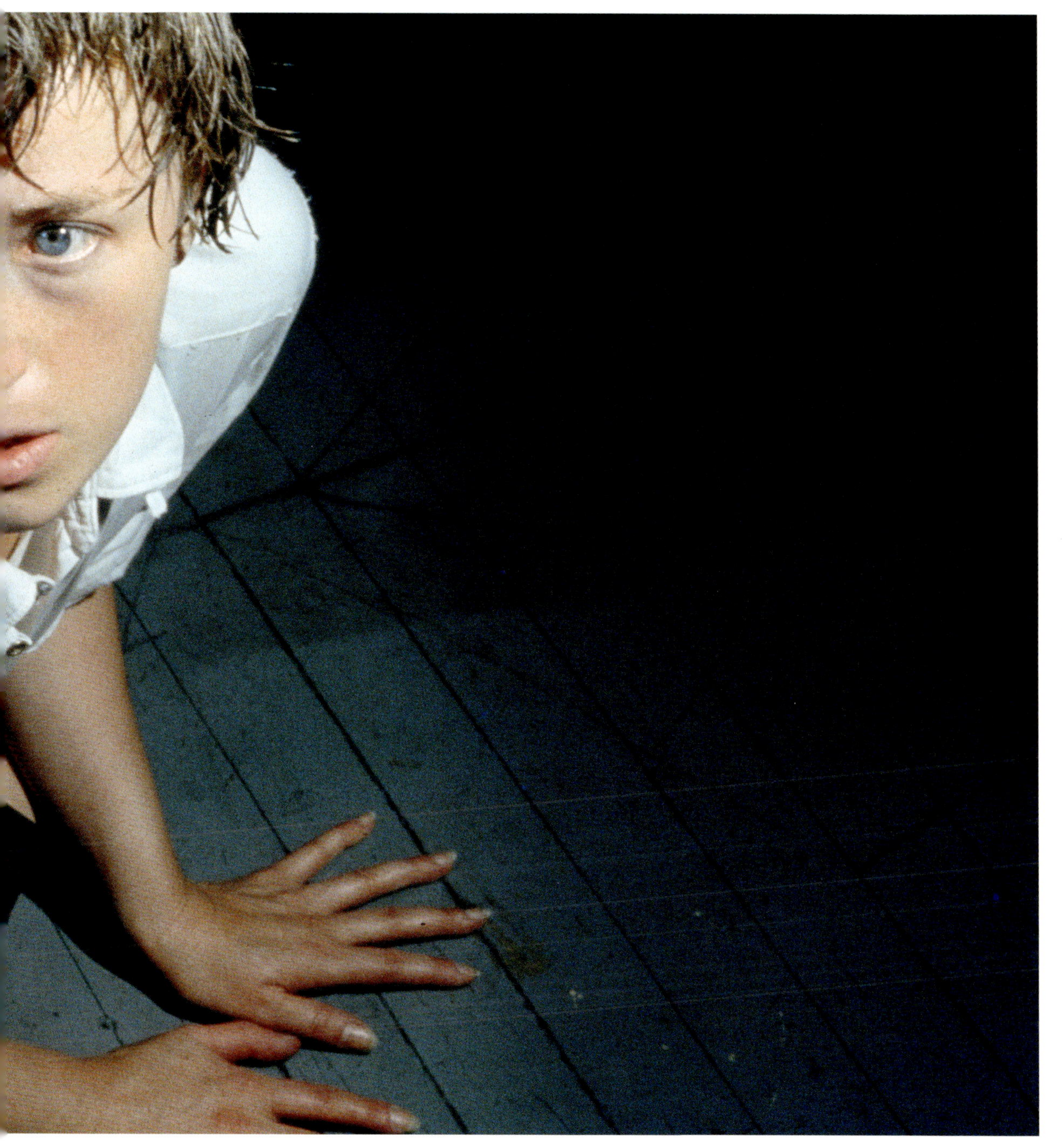

FIG. 19. Cindy Sherman (American, born 1954). Untitled #92. 1981. Chromogenic color print, 24 × 48" (61 × 121.9 cm). THE MUSEUM OF MODERN ART, NEW YORK. THE FELLOWS OF PHOTOGRAPHY FUND

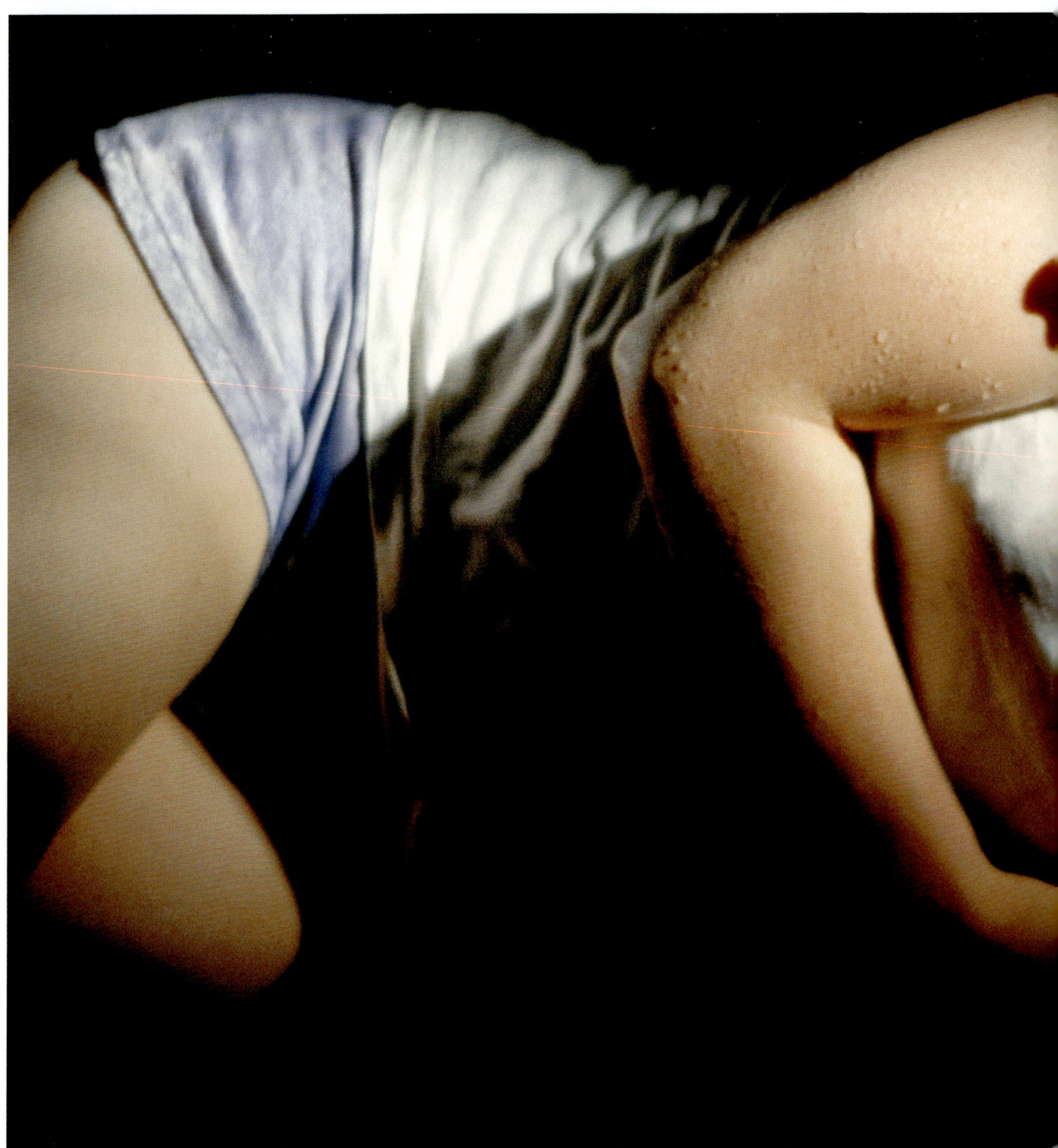

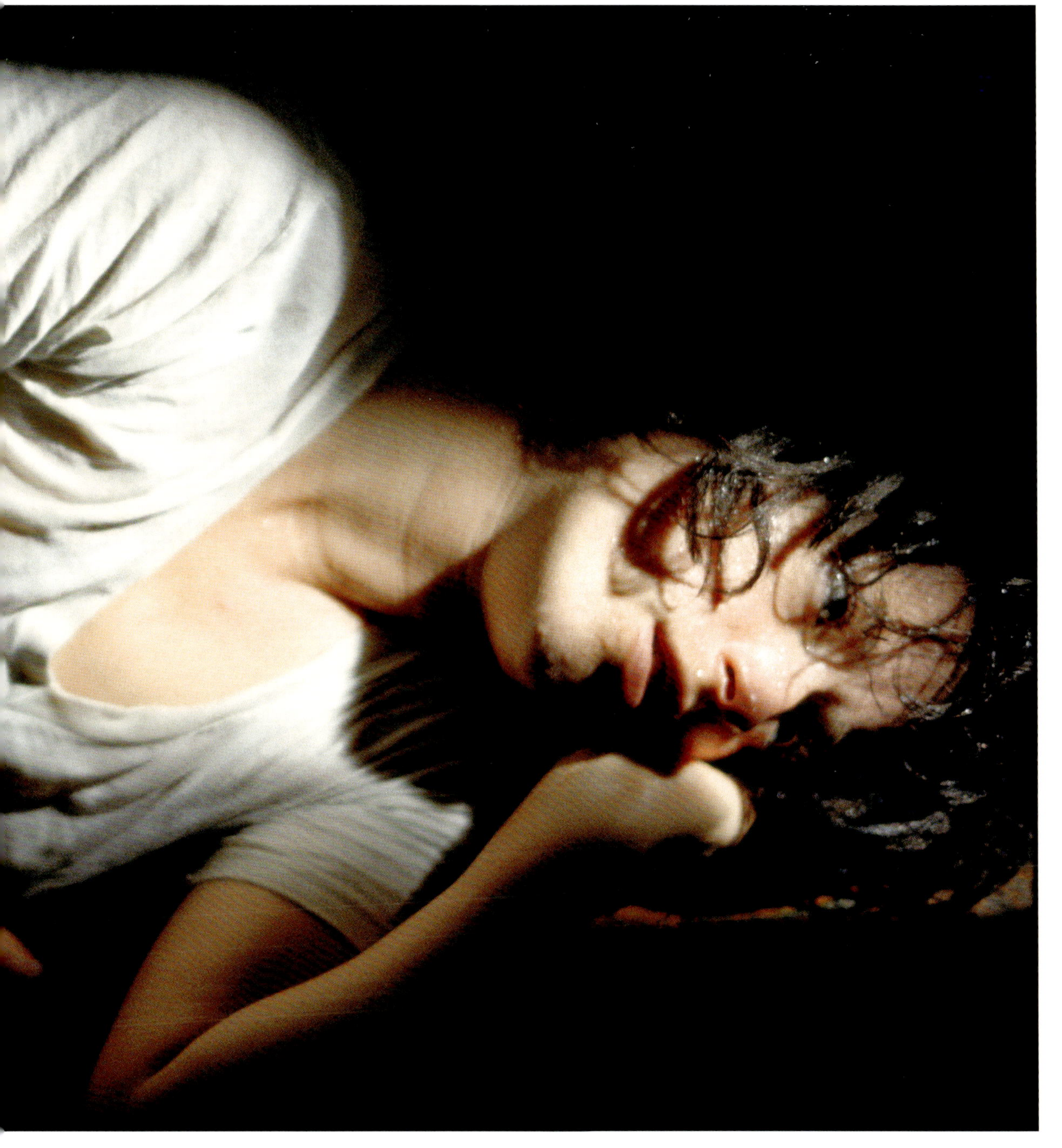

FIG. 20. Cindy Sherman (American, born 1954). Untitled #86. 1981. Chromogenic color print. 24 × 48" (61 × 121.9 cm)

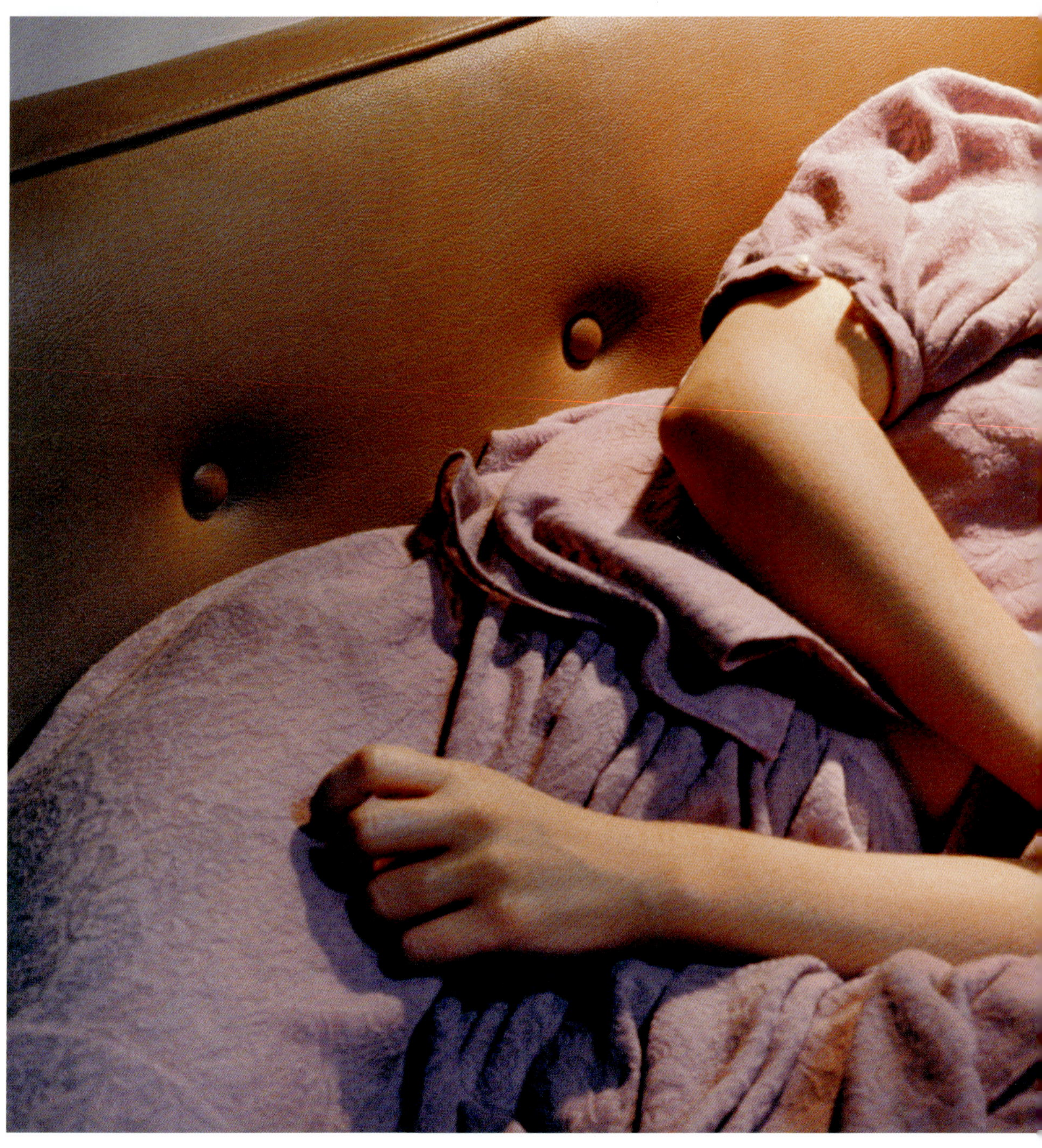

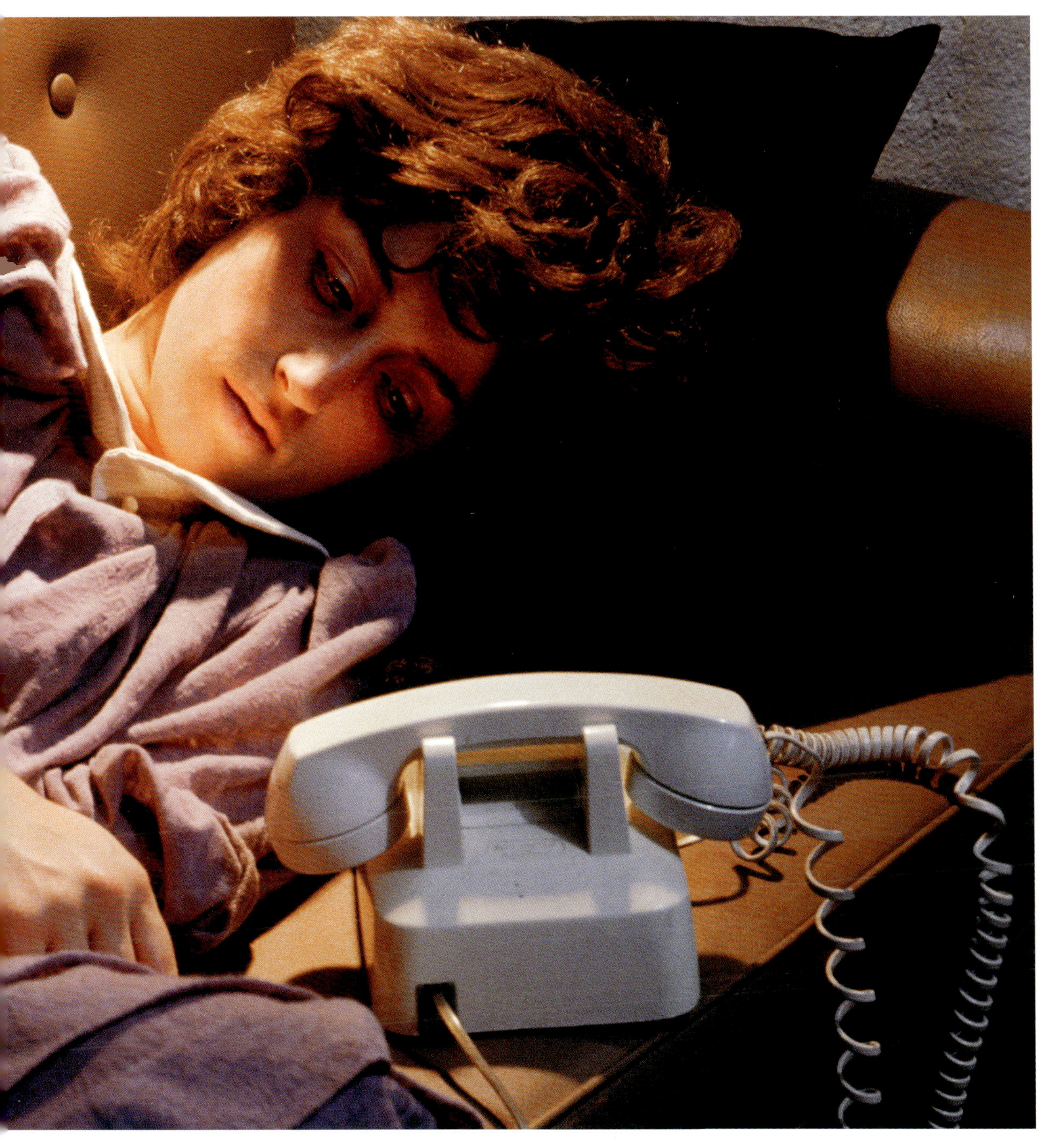

FIG. 21. Cindy Sherman (American, born 1954). Untitled #90. 1981. Chromogenic color print, 24 × 48" (61 × 121.9 cm)

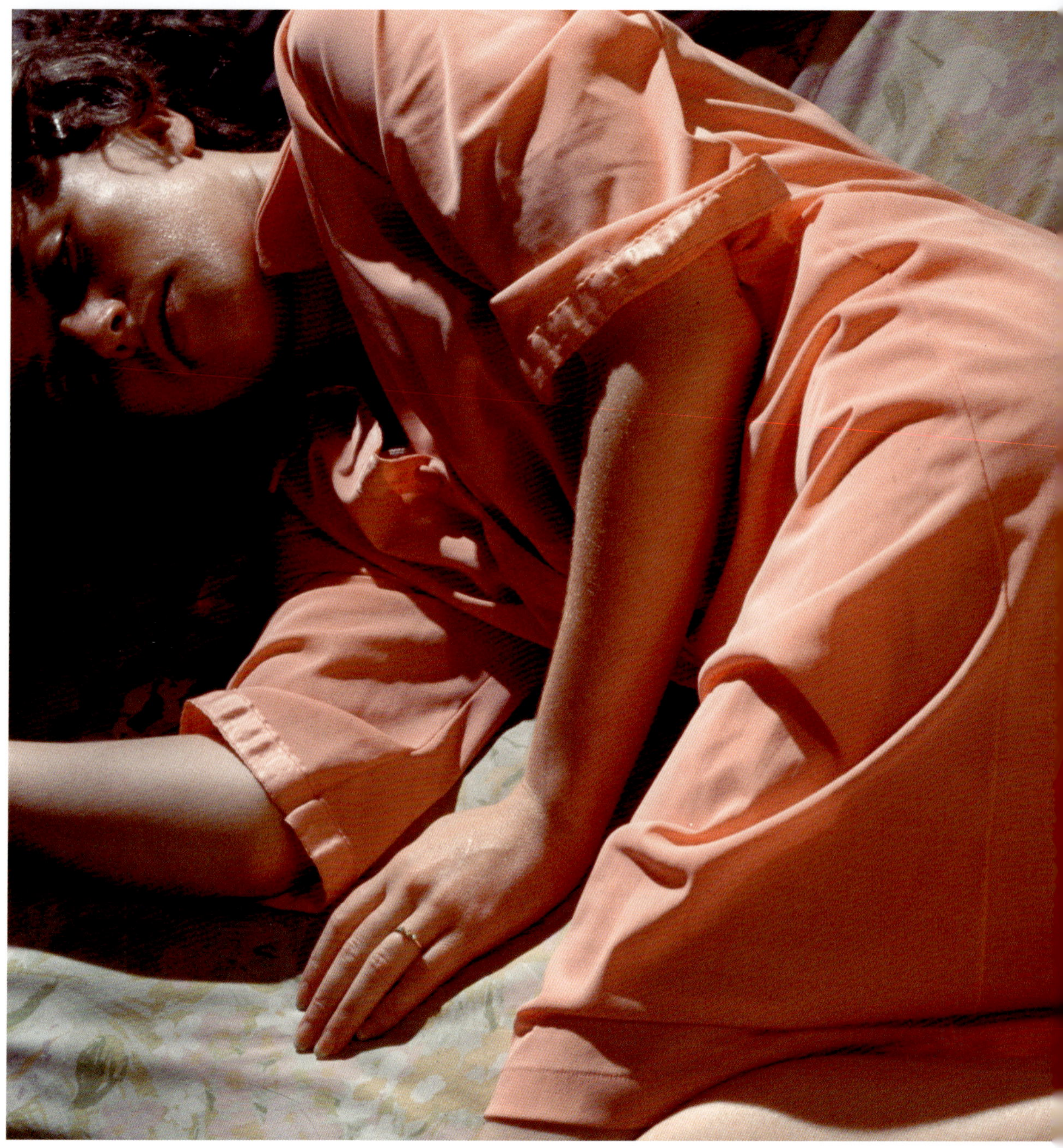

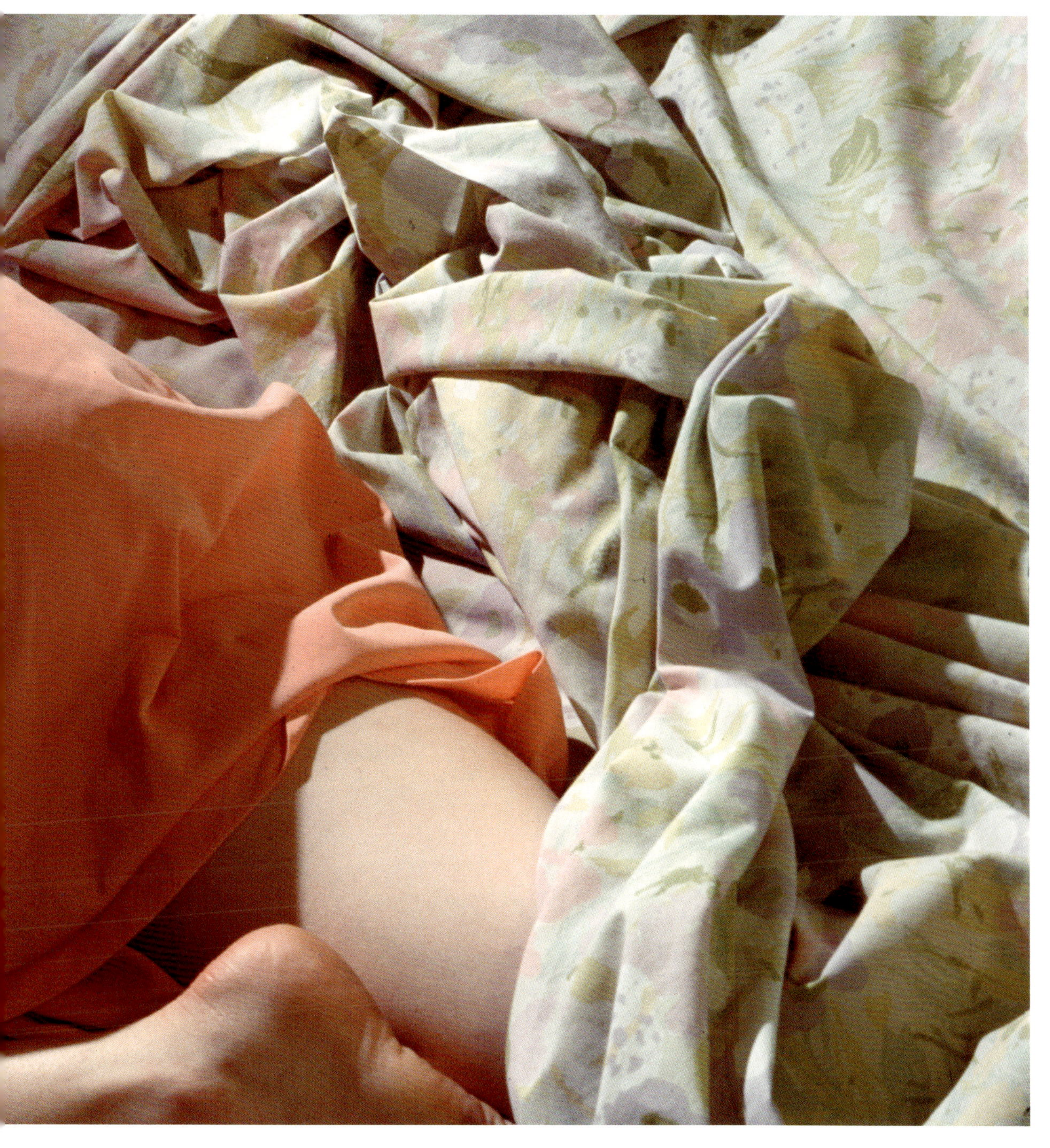

FIG. 22. Cindy Sherman (American, born 1954). Untitled #89. 1981. Chromogenic color print, 24 × 48" (61 × 121.9 cm)

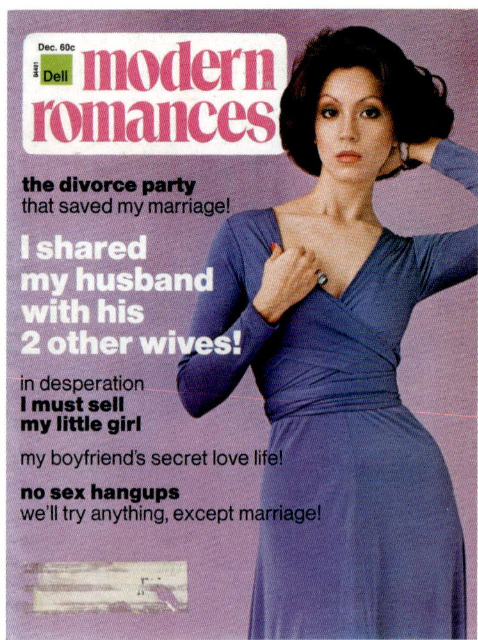

FIG. 23. Cover of *Modern Romances* magazine, December 1975

who were usually trapped or helpless victims **[FIGS. 23, 24]**. Judith Williamson observed that many of the characters in the Centerfolds "look as if they were trodden on by men."[16] In all of these pictures, the vulnerability of the women is exacerbated by the sense that they believe themselves to be alone.

None of the photographs ever ran in *Artforum* because Sischy, who was concerned the pictures looked "a little too close" to the pornographic images they sought to critique, feared that their irony would be lost on viewers.[17] Allegedly the only time Sischy rejected an artwork she had commissioned, this act of editorial censorship is in itself a fascinating part of the history of these photographs, attesting to their potency while raising the question of what made them so controversial. Among other things, the situation conjured up an earlier scandal in the pages of *Artforum*, which also involved a project by a female artist referencing the pornographic centerfold. In 1974 Lynda Benglis published her infamous *Artforum* ad: a two-page spread, paid for by her gallery, in which she appears nude, greased, and defiantly holding a large, double-ended dildo. Read alternately as a feminist statement and an indictment of the magazine's promotional tendencies, the image so shocked and offended *Artforum*'s own editors that several of them resigned. Although this controversy took place years before her tenure at *Artforum*, Sischy would certainly have been familiar with the incident and subsequent fallout; she may have been wary of repeating history.

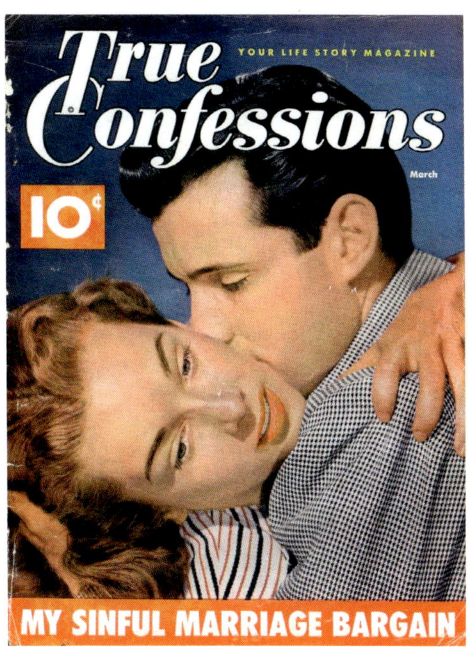

FIG. 24. Cover of *True Confessions* magazine, March 1952

Unlike the Untitled Film Stills, which rely on familiar, relatable characters and devices from across cinema, the Centerfolds were much more challenging, even disturbing, to many viewers when they were initially shown. "I was definitely trying to provoke in those pictures," Sherman recalled. "But it was more about provoking men into reassessing their assumptions when they look at pictures of women. I was thinking about vulnerability in a way that would make a male viewer feel uncomfortable—like seeing your daughter in a vulnerable state."[18] While some critics read the series as a satirical and critical appropriation of pornography, others commented on what they perceived to be violent overtones, going so far as to suggest that the photographs depicted rape victims. As Sherman would later note, "I got a lot of criticism for being 'anti-feminist' and 'turning the clock back' by showing these 'victims.'"[19] To fully understand the impact the Centerfolds had on viewers, it is helpful to compare them to the actual pornographic images they both allude to and problematize.

Playboy magazine, founded in 1953, established the practice of featuring a nude or scantily clad model in a double-page spread (and eventually a trifold) in each issue. Although the term *centerfold* had long been in use in the printers' trade to refer to the two-page spread at the center of a staple-bound magazine, *Playboy*'s publisher, Hugh Hefner, was responsible for establishing its now unavoidable prurient connotation. He sought to cultivate a wholesome, girl-next-door appearance for his centerfold models (known as "playmates"), specifying that they should have a "healthy, intelligent, American look—a young lady that looks like she might be a very efficient secretary or an undergrad at Vassar."[20] The magazine tried to make its centerfold models approachable by listing their jobs, activities, and hobbies, and by hinting at a storyline through props or furnishings that suggested "the presence of someone not in the picture." The overall aim was to convert "a straight pinup into an intimate interlude, something personal and special" **[FIG. 25]**.[21] (These innovations were a huge success: by the 1970s *Playboy*'s circulation was in the millions, cementing the magazine as a veritable American institution and sexual rite of passage for many young men. Today, its cultural import has all but evaporated with the proliferation of free porn websites; indeed, the Spring 2020 issue would be the magazine's last.) Sherman appropriated many of the visual codes and conventions of centerfold photographs, such as the horizontal format, recumbent pose, and overhead viewpoint. Many of the women in the Centerfolds (including the figure in *Untitled #96*) have the look of female coeds. Their poses mimic the distinctive, slightly awkward poses of centerfold models, the goal of which was to reveal as much skin as possible within the horizontal frame.[22] Despite these deliberate parallels, Sherman's photographs are also at odds with the flirtatious, come-hither demeanor of the typical centerfold pinup. Her women are instead remote, unavailable, and imbued with a sexualized vulnerability bordering on victimization. They don't look directly at the camera, but neither do they make themselves alluring in a passive way nor signal the "to-be-looked-at-ness" associated with the male gaze. Instead of inviting the viewer into the image as a willing participant, Sherman casts us as intrusive voyeurs.

The polarized reception of the Centerfolds was most likely influenced by the larger debates over pornography that were taking place at the time. In 1981 Andrea Dworkin published her groundbreaking book *Pornography: Men Possessing Women*, in which she argued that pornography objectifies and dehumanizes women, and denounced it as a form of violence. Dworkin and other anti-pornography feminists, including the legal scholar Catharine A. MacKinnon, pushed for legislation restricting pornography as a type of sex discrimination. Meanwhile, so-called sex-positive feminists condemned such views as promoting censorship and sexual repression. These academic debates, sometimes referred to as the "feminist sex wars," filtered down into popular culture. Coincidentally, the same year Sherman created the Centerfolds, the J. Geils Band released its hit single "Centerfold," about a man who discovers that his former teenage crush is featured in a "girlie magazine."

If the Centerfolds hit a cultural nerve at the time of their creation, they remain irreducible to a single reading today. This quality is part of what makes *Untitled #96* and the other images in the series such compelling and enduring works of art. Rather than telling us what to think, the photographs powerfully elicit our own projections and interpretations. As Williamson writes:

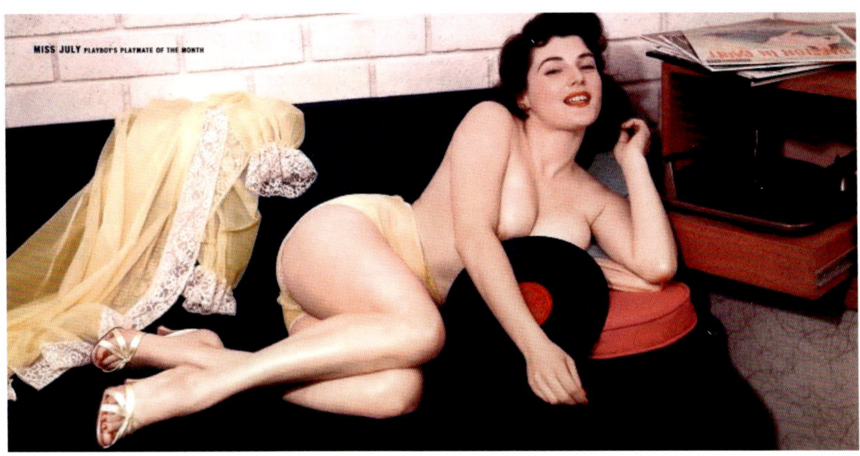

FIG. 25. Centerfold in *Playboy*, July 1957

> *Untitled #96* . . . shows precisely the way that we read into [the girl's] fundamentally "unreadable" face some emotional response which is both very definite, and entirely ambiguous. She looks thoughtful, but whether she is happy or unhappy, worried or perfectly all right we have no clue. She looks, exactly, uncertain. Yet between the newspaper cutting and her face there is an endless production of significance which seems inevitable (it's always already started) and almost clear in its vagueness. Happy or unhappy, anxious or zoned out. Either way, her expression is an index of something and someone else, something we don't know about but which everything in the frame points to.[23]

Arguably, that unknown "something or someone else" is the viewer. And, with meaning tantalizingly offered only to be frustrated, all we're left with is our own response to the image—our own memories, desires, fantasies, and fears.

—

While none of the Centerfolds ran in *Artforum* as originally intended, Sherman would eventually accept a different commission from the magazine, and the resulting artist's project was published in the December 1985 issue **[FIG. 26]**. In this image, spread over one and a half pages, the artist appears as a bearded old man being photographed by a male photographer, also played by Sherman. The figures, at once elfin and monstrous, wear fake noses and other prosthetics.

ART ON LOCATION

The criticism that views Cindy Sherman's role-playing photography as a deconstruction of female stereotypes (like a latter-day August Sander project, but with media images of women replacing his cataloguing of the German people), while applicable, now seems too academic and willful for the transvestism that Sherman has been staging of late. Her recent transformational characters, whether created with expressive makeup, lighting, and shadows or with the use of masks, whether she appears as a snout-faced pig or as a bearded man, have such a stylized, out-of-time, out-of-sex quality that they leave the politics of our time and enter the magical time of make-believe.

Fantasy is as much a part of Sherman's art as is a theoretical analysis of the roles we play, and of the selves we're offered as models. Even in her earlier "film stills" series, 1977–80, about movie typecasting, there's a deeply personal thread that ties these public pictures to her psychological apparatus. For example, the story behind the famous photo that looks like an appropriated scene from *Bus Stop* goes as follows: Sherman was on a car trip with her mother and father. In the car were wigs, outfits, miscellaneous props, and her camera, which she'd brought along to bide the time. They were driving along one of those roads in Arizona with a few bitty trees, and an occasional pond that looks like a large puddle from a moving car, when they turned a bend for more of the same. Sherman asked to stop the car, put on an outfit, set up the camera, ran into the frame of scenery she wanted, and told her father when to click the camera. The result: a glamorous, romantic, Hollywood image. They played this game along the way at various spots. Creating a different life from the one we have in the back seat is something we all do in our imaginations, but instead of letting it slip away, Sherman stops it frame by frame—whether gorgeous or battered—to see what it would look and feel like. She knows that photography is the modern equivalent of the mask and that it offers an opportunity to show all of our selves—except one. This is modern-day kabuki that she's performing. What Cindy Sherman the photographer "really" looks like would hurt the magic as much as seeing a kabuki star out of costume and in the bank.

The studio drama performed here by three Cindy Shermans—you have to include the one offstage taking the picture, whose trace is left by the cord of the light meter—is the popular theme of photographer and subject in a primal battle over control. This is an archaic fight, both pre- and post-Modern. The spirit inside the tripod could change it into a club at any moment. The old man has had it with the photographer's tricks and the photographer is passively goading him even further so he can get the picture he wants.
—INGRID SISCHY

"On Location" project for *Artforum* by Cindy Sherman, 1985. Montage created from two 35 mm. color slides.

4

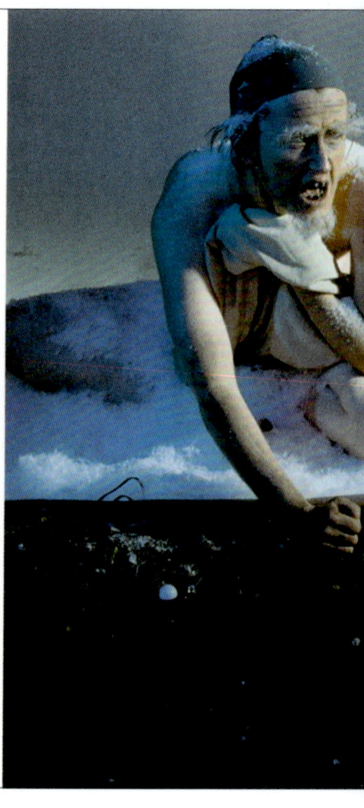

They bear similarity to the make-believe characters she had begun to explore earlier that year in a series dubbed the Fairy Tales (itself originally commissioned for *Vanity Fair* magazine but never published) **[FIG. 27]**. In the *Artforum* image, the old man is nude, save for a sheet that he clutches to himself, and covered in fake snow. His face and body contorted in anguish, he howls, revealing a mouthful of rotting teeth, and pounds his fist on the ground in protest. Meanwhile, the photographer at his tripod appears blithely indifferent to the old man's suffering, concerned only with getting the perfect shot. The image brings to mind a fashion shoot in which (usually young female) models are forced to endure any number of discomforts to accommodate the whims of editorial direction. However, by replacing the female "victims" that had appeared in the Centerfolds with a decrepit, grotesque old man, Sherman calls attention to the exploitative conditions of the modeling industry without running the risk of reiterating its objectification of women. At the same time, she pointedly suggests how sexism and ageism play into the reception of such images, whether they appear on the magazine page or gallery wall.

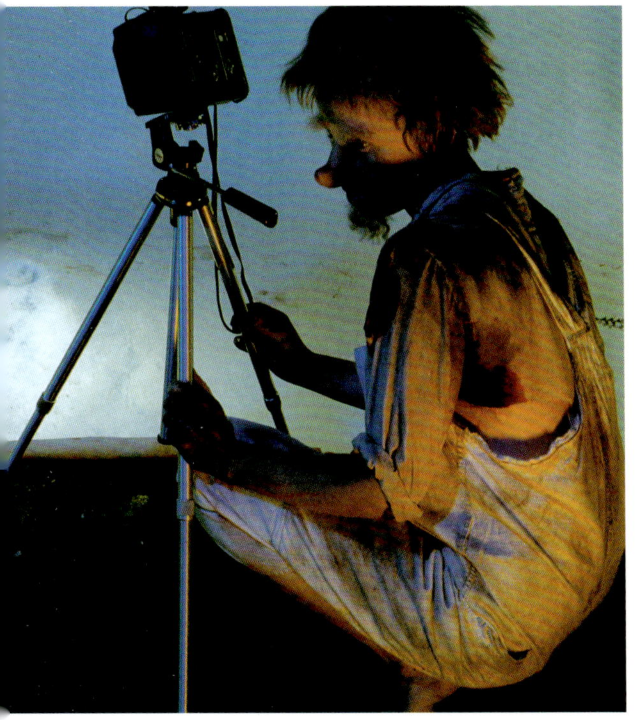

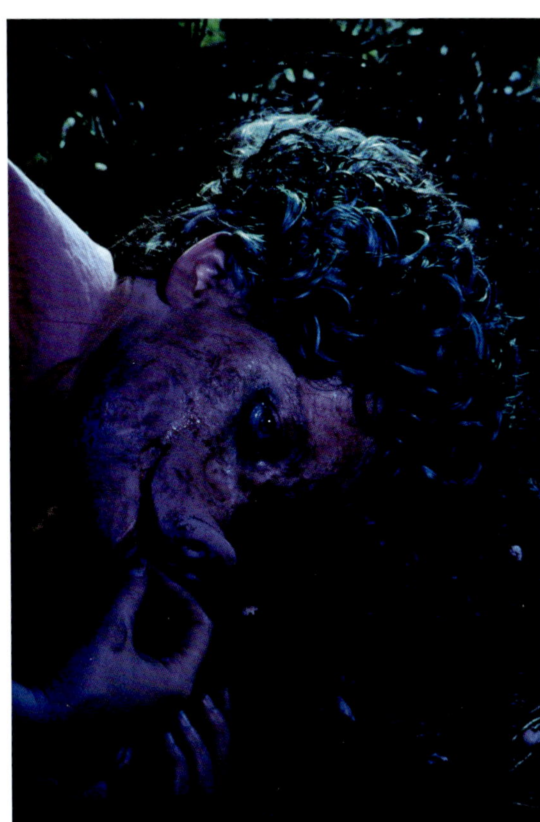

FIG. 26. Left: Cindy Sherman's project in *Artforum*, December 1985

FIG. 27. Right: Cindy Sherman (American, born 1954). Untitled #140. 1985. Chromogenic color print, 72 ½ × 48 ⅜" (184.2 × 122.9 cm)

Looking back, the Centerfolds hinted at a number of future directions Sherman's work would take. She continued to mine the theme of the pornographic pinup the following year in a suite of four photographs (*Untitled #97–#100*), known as the Pink Robe series, in which she wears (or covers herself with) a hot pink chenille bathrobe and nothing else **[FIGS. 28, 29]**. According to Sherman, "The pictures were meant to look like a model just after she'd been photographed for a centerfold."[24] Glaring out at the viewer with a matter-of-fact directness, she dares us to confront the centerfold model not as a consumable sex object but as a real person. The artist would again delve into the topic of pornography for a series christened the Sex Pictures (1992), in which she created raunchy and pornographic scenes using medical mannequins that she had

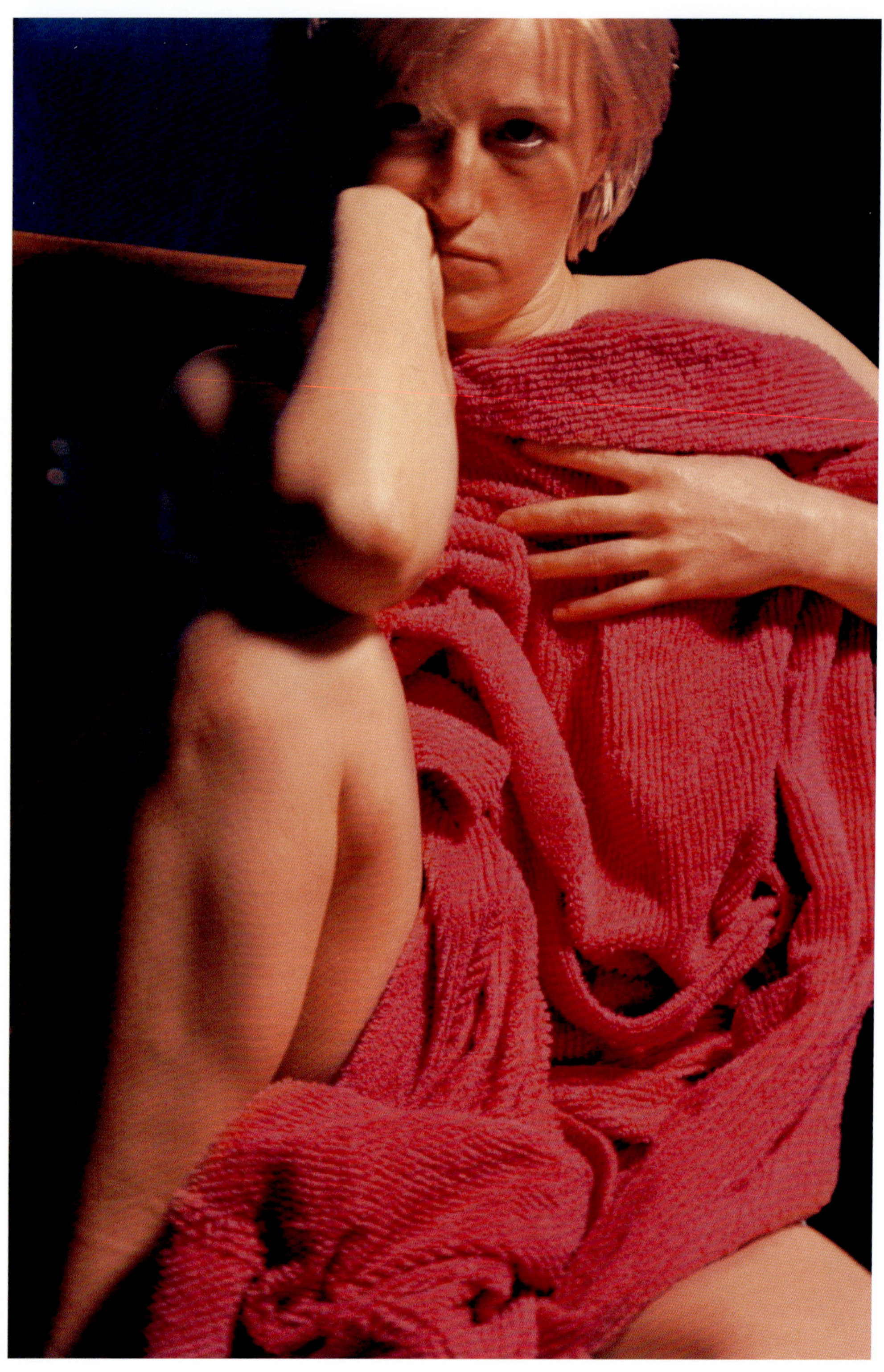

FIG. 28. Cindy Sherman (American, born 1954). Untitled #97. 1982. Chromogenic color print, 45 9⁄32 × 29 29⁄32" (115 × 76 cm)

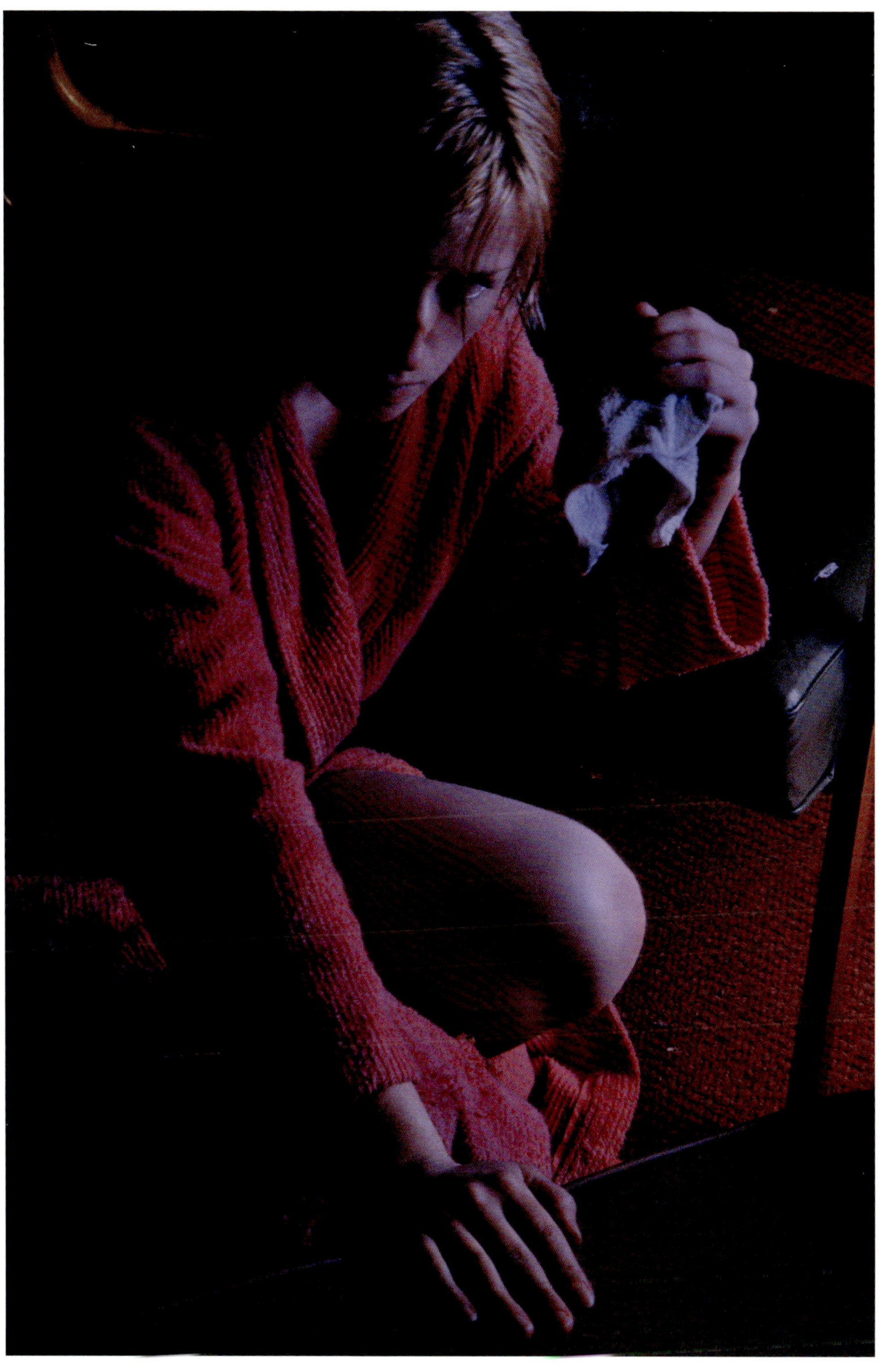

FIG. 29. Cindy Sherman (American, born 1954). Untitled #100. 1982. Chromogenic color print, 45 9⁄32 × 29 29⁄32" (115 × 76 cm)

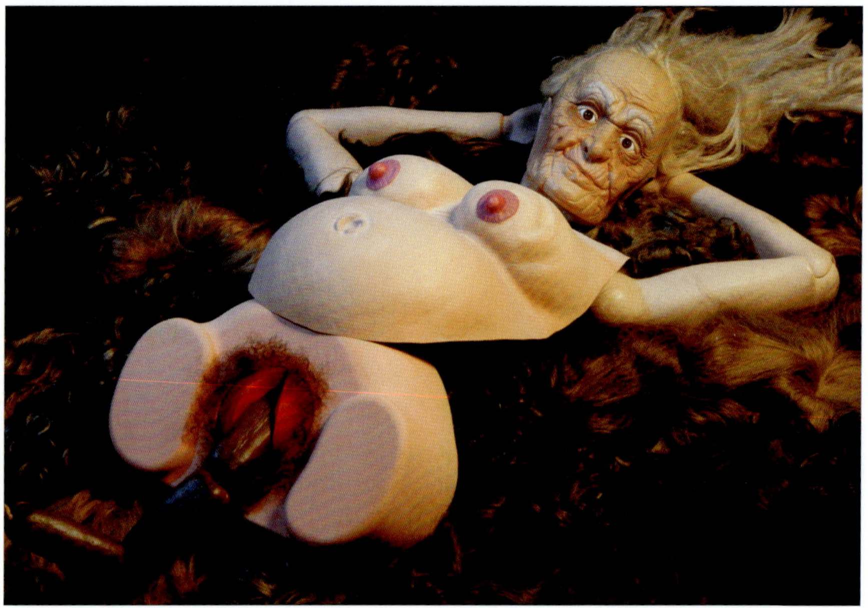

FIG. 30. Cindy Sherman (American, born 1954). Untitled #250. 1992. Chromogenic color print, 49 ⅜" x 6' 2½" (125.5 x 189.2 cm). THE MUSEUM OF MODERN ART, NEW YORK. GIFT OF THE DANNHEISSER FOUNDATION

dismembered and modified **[FIG. 30]**. Called "the unsexiest sex pictures ever made" by the critic Jerry Saltz, the images are at once sexually explicit and completely unerotic.[25] They were in part a response to the National Endowment for the Arts censorship wars that were wracking the art world at the time. (One of the most infamous episodes from this period occurred in 1989, when twenty-five conservative senators cosigned a letter demanding reforms to the NEA, largely in response to controversial exhibitions that had recently received funding from the agency, including a Robert Mapplethorpe retrospective featuring sadomasochist imagery.)

Magazines—as subject matter and medium—would remain central to Sherman's subsequent work. Throughout the 1980s and '90s, the artist accepted commissions from publications such as *Interview*, *Vogue Paris*, and *Harper's Bazaar* for advertisements and editorial spreads in which she wears clothing by high-end labels like Jean-Paul Gaultier and Comme des Garçons **[FIG. 31]**. But rather than projecting glamour, Sherman appears frumpy, awkward, tacky, and even psychotic. "I'm disgusted with how people get themselves to look beautiful," she remarked. "I'm much more fascinated with the other side. . . . I was trying to make fun of fashion."[26] These "anti-advertisements"—collectively referred to as the Fashion series—knowingly walk a fine line between criticizing the fashion industry

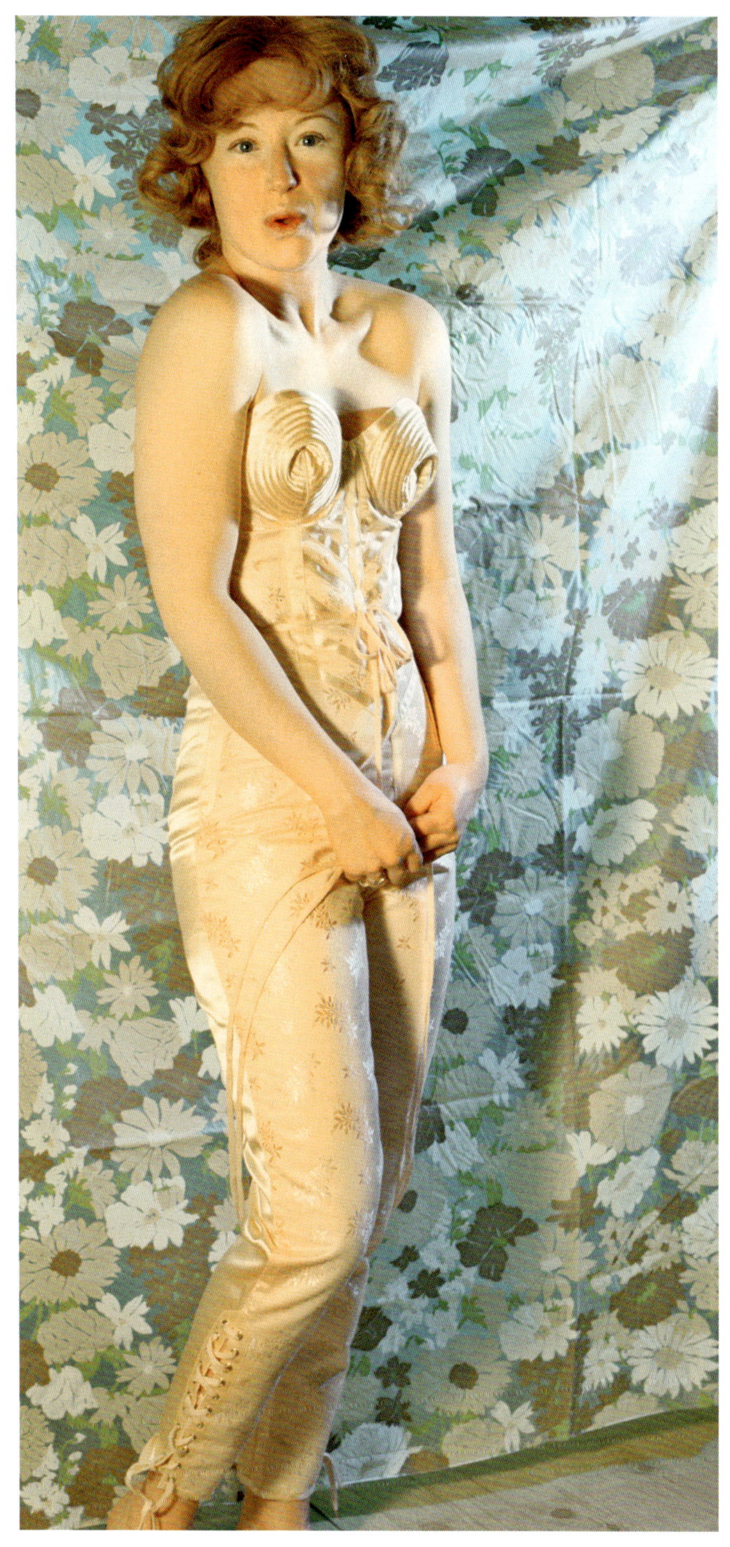

FIG. 31. Cindy Sherman (American, born 1954). *Untitled # 131*. 1983. Chromogenic color print, 35 × 16 ½" (89 × 41.9 cm). THE MUSEUM OF MODERN ART, NEW YORK. JOEL AND ANNE EHRENKRANZ FUND

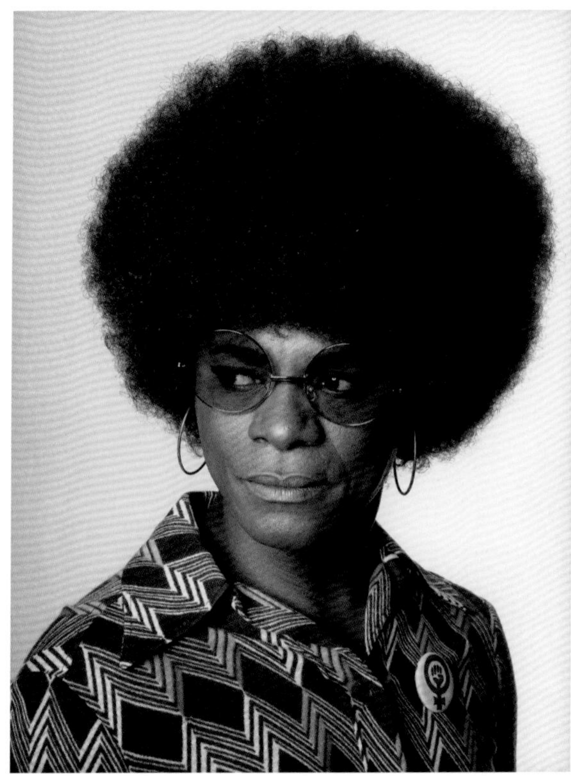

FIG. 32. Samuel Fosso (French and Central African, born Cameroon 1962). Untitled, from the series African Spirits. 2008. Gelatin silver print, 64 ⅛ × 48 1⁄16" (162.8 × 122 cm). THE MUSEUM OF MODERN ART, NEW YORK. THE FAMILY OF MAN FUND

and fueling its voracious appetite for novelty and sensationalism. The artist has since gone on to collaborate on ad campaigns for brands including Marc Jacobs, Balenciaga, Louis Vuitton, and MAC Cosmetics, and most recently she created a project for the March 2016 issue of *Harper's Bazaar* inspired by Instagram street-style fashion influencers. In 2017 Sherman became a social media influencer in her own right when she began posting caricature-like, often freakish-looking selfies to her Instagram account, using Facetune and other photo-editing apps to manipulate her facial features and add filters and effects.

With the Centerfolds, Sherman outlines a transition from woman as object to woman as subject—probing the psychological effects of images of women and asking us to reflect on the violence, as well as the distinct pleasures, of contemporary visual culture. While certain reference points that shaped the initial reception of *Untitled #96* nearly forty years ago may have lost some of their valence, the photograph continues to resonate deeply with viewers today. It is interesting to

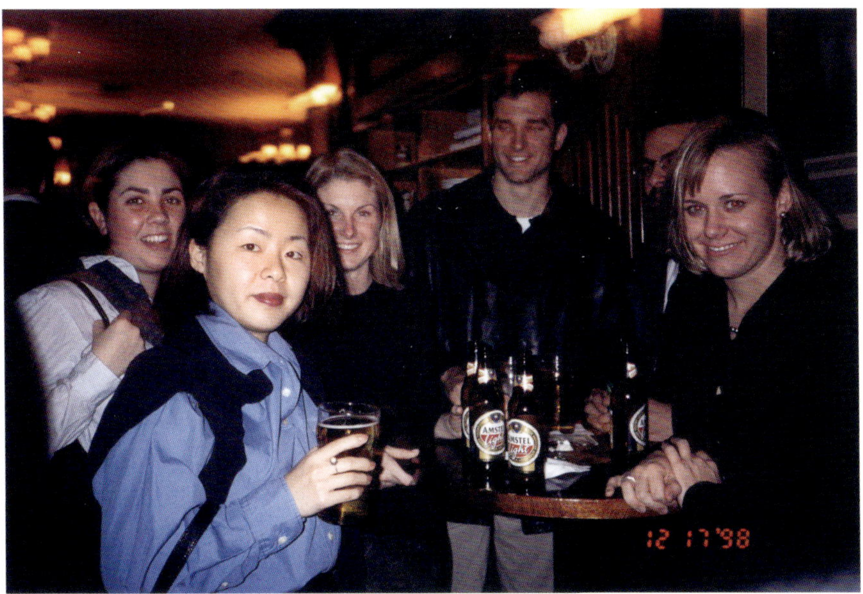

FIG. 33. Nikki S. Lee (American, born Korea 1970). *The Yuppie Project (12)*. 1998. Chromogenic color print, dimensions variable

consider, for example, how the meaning of *Untitled #96* and the rest of the Centerfolds series changes when examined in the wake of the #MeToo movement. Sherman was in fact one of the signatories to an open letter published by We Are Not Surprised—a collective of women, transgender, and gender-nonconforming artists and arts workers that formed in October 2017 to protest sexism and sexual harassment in the art world. The letter was a response to recent allegations of abuse and discrimination in museums, art magazines, and other institutions, including *Artforum*. As the mainstream art world has struggled in recent years to become more inclusive—not just in terms of gender but also race, ethnicity, nationality, and geography—Sherman's pioneering explorations of representation, power, and identity (along with those of some of her contemporaries, such as Carrie Mae Weems and Yasumasa Morimura) continue to inspire and inform a new generation of artists, as witnessed in the works of Martine Gutierrez, Nikki S. Lee, Genevieve Gaignard, Samuel Fosso, and Amalia Ulman. These image-makers have used performative modes of self-portraiture to consider the politics of race and ethnicity as well as queer and transgender identity **[FIGS. 32, 33]**. This more recent work has inherited, even as it expands and transforms, the legacy of Sherman's Centerfolds, pointing out the ways in which images participate in unjust power relationships—and attesting to art's capacity to confront and thus potentially alter them.

NOTES

1. The only body of work that Cindy Sherman has titled is the series Untitled Film Stills. The rest of her series are untitled, although many of them have been published extensively with informal series titles for ease of reference. These titles are referred to in this book for clarity, but they are not proper titles. Sherman has also not numbered her photographs. The numbers that appear after "untitled" are inventory numbers assigned by her gallery, Metro Pictures. Since the numbered titles have been widely published, we have chosen to include the numbers in this book for consistency and, again, for ease of reference. In running text but not in figure captions, we italicize these numbered titles the way we would any other (though technically Sherman's works are untitled).

2. Cindy Sherman, in *Cindy Sherman: Nobody's Here but Me*, directed by Mark Stokes, a Cinecontact production for BBC and the Arts Council of Great Britain, aired April 24, 1994, on BBC 2, https://www.youtube.com/watch?v=UXKNuWtXZ_U.

3. Sherman, in Carol Vogel, "Cindy Sherman Unmasked," *New York Times*, February 16, 2012.

4. Douglas Crimp, *Pictures: An Exhibition of the Work of Troy Brauntuch, Jack Goldstein, Sherrie Levine, Robert Longo, Philip Smith*, exh. cat. (New York: Committee for the Visual Arts, 1977), p. 3.

5. Sherman, in Calvin Tomkins, "Her Secret Identities," *New Yorker*, May 15, 2000, p. 78.

6. Craig Owens, "The Allegorical Impulse: Toward a Theory of Postmodernism, Part 2" (1980) in *Cindy Sherman*, October Files 6, ed. Johanna Burton (Cambridge, Mass.: MIT Press, 2006), p. 18.

7. Rosalind Krauss, "Cindy Sherman: Untitled" (1993) in Burton, *Cindy Sherman*, p. 98.

8. Crimp, "The Photographic Activity of Postmodernism" (1980) in Burton, *Cindy Sherman*, p. 35.

9. Judith Williamson, "A Piece of the Action: Images of 'Woman' in the Photography of Cindy Sherman" (1983/1986) in Burton, *Cindy Sherman*, pp. 52, 43.

10. Ibid., pp. 39–40.

11. Ibid., p. 44.

12. Sherman, "'80s Then: Cindy Sherman Talks to David Frankel," *Artforum*, March 2003, p. 54.

13. Dan Graham, "Interview with Dan Graham by Rodney Graham" (2008) in *Dan Graham: Beyond* (Los Angeles: Museum of Contemporary Art, Los Angeles; Cambridge, Mass.: MIT Press, 2009), p. 104.

14. Ingrid Sischy, "Letter from the Editor," *Artforum*, February 1980, p. 26.

15. The prints' size and horizontal orientation also allude to CinemaScope, a wide-screen movie format that was promoted by a number of major film studios during the 1950s.

16. Williamson, "Piece of the Action," p. 42.

17. Ingrid Sischy, in Tomkins, "Her Secret Identities," p. 78.

18. Sherman, in ibid., p. 79.

19. Sherman, in Paul Taylor, "Cindy Sherman," *Flash Art*, October/November 1985, p. 79.

20. Hugh Hefner to *Playboy* photographers, memorandum, 1956, in Steven Watts, *Mr. Playboy: Hugh Hefner and the American Dream* (New York: John Wiley & Sons, 2008), p. 117.

21. Hefner to Russ Meyer, letter, March 1, 1955, in Dave Hickey, introduction to *Playboy: The Complete Centerfolds* (San Francisco: Chronicle Books, 2007), n.p.

22. See Kelly Dennis, *Art/Porn: A History of Seeing and Touching* (Oxford: Berg, 2009).

23. Williamson, "Piece of the Action," p. 42.

24. Sherman, in Taylor, "Cindy Sherman," p. 79.

25. Jerry Saltz, "Cindy Sherman: Becoming," *New York*, February 10, 2012, https://nymag.com/fashion/12/spring/cindy-sherman-2012-2/.

26. Sherman, "Cindy Sherman's Tales of Terror," interview by Larry Frascella, *Aperture*, Summer 1986, p. 49.

FOR FURTHER READING

Burton, Johanna, ed. *Cindy Sherman*. October Files 6. Cambridge, Mass.: MIT Press, 2006.

Cruz, Amanda, Elizabeth A. T. Smith, and Amelia Jones. *Cindy Sherman: Retrospective*. Exh. cat. New York: Thames & Hudson, 1997.

Eklund, Douglas. *The Pictures Generation, 1974–1984*. Exh. cat. New York: Metropolitan Museum of Art; New Haven: Yale University Press, 2009.

Galassi, Peter, ed. *Cindy Sherman: The Complete Untitled Film Stills*. New York: The Museum of Modern Art, 2003.

Krauss, Rosalind, and Norman Bryson. *Cindy Sherman, 1975–1993*. New York: Rizzoli, 1993.

Phillips, Lisa, ed. *Cindy Sherman*. Exh. cat. New York: Whitney Museum of American Art, 1987.

Phillips, Lisa. *Cindy Sherman: Centerfolds*. Exh. cat. New York: Skarstedt Fine Art, 2003.

Respini, Eva, ed. *Cindy Sherman*. Exh. cat. New York: The Museum of Modern Art, 2012.

Produced by the Department of Publications
The Museum of Modern Art, New York

Edited by Jackie Neudorf
Series designed by Miko McGinty and Rita Jules
Layout by Amanda Washburn
Production by Matthew Pimm
Proofread by Maria Marchenkova
Printed and bound by Ofset Yapimevi, Istanbul

Typeset in Ideal Sans
Printed on 150 gsm Magno Satin

Published by The Museum of Modern Art
11 West 53 Street
New York, NY 10019-5497
www.moma.org

ISBN: 978-1-63345-118-6

Distributed in the United States and Canada by
ARTBOOK | D.A.P.
75 Broad Street
Suite 630
New York, NY 10004
www.artbook.com

Distributed outside the United States and Canada by
Thames & Hudson Ltd
181A High Holborn
London WC1V 7QX
www.thamesandhudson.com

Printed and bound in Turkey

PHOTOGRAPH CREDITS

In reproducing the images contained in this publication, the Museum obtained the permission of the rights holders whenever possible. If the Museum could not locate the rights holders, notwithstanding good-faith efforts, it requests that any contact information concerning such rights holders be forwarded so that they may be contacted for future editions.

All works by Cindy Sherman © Cindy Sherman

Courtesy Artists Space, New York: fig. 12. © Center for Creative Photography, Arizona Board of Regents; Department of Imaging Services, The Museum of Modern Art, New York: fig. 16. © Walker Evans Archive, The Metropolitan Museum of Art, New York; image source Art Resource, New York: fig. 14. © S. Fosso, courtesy JM. Patras/Paris; Department of Imaging Services, The Museum of Modern Art, New York: fig. 32. © 2017 Dan Graham; Department of Imaging Services, The Museum of Modern Art, New York, photo by Thomas Griesel: fig. 18. © Nikki S. Lee, courtesy Sikkema Jenkins & Co., New York: fig. 33. Courtesy the artist and Metro Pictures, New York: figs. 6, 7, 10, 11, 20–22, 27–29. Courtesy MGM Media Licensing; Some Like It Hot © 1959 Metro-Goldwyn-Mayer Studios Inc. All rights reserved: fig. 15. Department of Imaging Services, The Museum of Modern Art, New York: fig. 30; photo by Jonathan Muzikar: frontispiece; photos by John Wronn: figs. 1–5, 17, 19, 31. © Richard Prince; courtesy Gagosian: fig. 13. Photo courtesy Georgia Scherman Projects and the artist: fig. 8. "On Location: Cindy Sherman's Camera Kabuki" © Ingrid Sischy, originally published in *Artforum*, December 1985: fig. 26. © 2020 Marsie, Emanuelle, Damon and Andrew Scharlatt – Hannah Wilke Collection and Archive, Los Angeles; Department of Imaging Services, The Museum of Modern Art, New York: fig. 9.

TRUSTEES OF THE MUSEUM OF MODERN ART